Fred J. Hums School

92   447
AND   Newman, Shirlee P
        Marian Anderson:
        Lady from Philadelphia

92   447
AND

    Newman, Shirlee P

AUTHOR   Marian Anderson:

TITLE

   Lady from Philadelphia

DATE DUE	BORROWER'S NAME	ROOM NUMBER
JUN 75	JUN 76	
APR 2	Sharrell Y. Ligon	O
APR 21	renewed	O.

Marian Anderson:
LADY FROM PHILADELPHIA

Marian Anderson:
LADY FROM PHILADELPHIA

by

SHIRLEE P. NEWMAN

THE WESTMINSTER PRESS

Philadelphia

Photograph, page 23, courtesy of Roland Hayes.
Photograph, page 116, courtesy of *Look* magazine.
Photograph, page 147, courtesy of S. Hurok—A United Nations Photo.
All other photographs courtesy of S. Hurok.

Grateful acknowledgment is made to the Radio Corporation of America for excerpts from Vincent Sheean's textpiece on Marian Anderson, copyright ©1965 Radio Corporation of America; and to The Curtis Publishing Company for excerpts from *My Life in a White World*, by Marian Anderson, as told to Emily Kimbrough, originally published in the *Ladies' Home Journal*, copyright ©1960 The Curtis Publishing Company.

LIBRARY OF CONGRESS CATALOG CARD No. 66–10933

PUBLISHED BY THE WESTMINSTER PRESS ®
PHILADELPHIA, PENNSYLVANIA

PRINTED IN THE UNITED STATES OF AMERICA

For Paula

W E BELIEVE everyone has a gift for something, even if the gift is that of being a good friend. Young people should try and set a goal for themselves, and see that everything they do has some relation to the ultimate attainment of that goal. The degree with which they lend themselves to it shows the mettle of which they are made.

Marian Anderson

Marianna Farm
Danbury, Connecticut
April, 1965

CHAPTER

1

THE sun burned down on the cobblestone streets and brick sidewalks of Philadelphia that summer day in 1919, but teen-aged Marian Anderson, waiting on the corner for a trolley, hardly felt the heat. As the big green streetcar jolted to a stop, she sprang up the steps, smiled at the perspiring motorman, and dropped a coin into the fare box.

The car lurched forward, and Marian made her way past men and women crowded together on either side of the aisle, talking about the humidity, fanning themselves with straw hats or folded newspapers.

A stout woman sitting in the back moved over to make room for Marian. "My, you look cheerful for such a scorcher!" she said.

"Thank you." Marian squeezed into the empty seat and smoothed down the collar of her freshly ironed blouse. Who cared if it was hot? This was the day she had been looking forward to for most of her life—today she was going to enroll in the music school uptown! As the trolley jangled in and out of the narrow streets, she began to hum softly.

To Marian, singing was as natural as speaking. In fact, she would rather sing. She had been able to carry a tune since high chair days, and when she was about seven she had joined the junior choir at the Union Baptist Church near her home in South Philadelphia. She and Viola Johnson, another girl in the choir, became friends, and one Sunday they sang "The

9

Lord Is My Shepherd" in duet. Viola chose to sing the soprano and Marian the alto.

"Viola's voice sounded like skimmed milk," Marian's father told her mother. "Marian's voice was like corned beef and cabbage."

Indeed, Marian sang low notes so well that visitors from other churches took word of the "Baby Contralto" back to their own congregations, and before long, she was invited to sing in churches all over the city.

She'd been a quiet child with a thin face. Now, as a teen-ager, she was tall and graceful. Her face, heart-shaped, and with suggestions of dimples in her cheeks, was framed by long hair falling to her shoulders in gentle waves. Her eyes were large, dark, luminous, and when she sang, they brightened with sparks of joy. From the beginning, music was Marian Anderson's life.

Marian's inborn love of music also showed itself in forms other than singing. Looking out of the trolley window, she noticed they were passing the pawnshop around the corner from where she used to live. She smiled, recalling how, when she was six and no taller than the hydrant in front of the shop, she'd spied a violin hanging in the cluttered window. Just like the one the man plays in church, she'd thought. She could still remember the jingle of the bells dangling from the knob as she pushed open the door. It was dark inside, and the jumble of merchandise was covered with soot.

"P—please, Mister," she said to the pawnbroker peering down at her through thick tortoise-rimmed spectacles, "how much would I need to buy the violin?"

"Three dollars and forty-five cents," he replied, summoning as businesslike a tone as he could, considering the size of the customer. "Do you think you can afford it?"

"No. That must be an awful lot of money." She backed out the door carefully, to avoid disturbing the bells again. "But I'll try to earn it," she added.

The next day, her mother's scrub pail swinging from her

10

arm, Marian reached up and rang a neighbor's doorbell. "I'll rub and scrub, and make your steps clean," she recited, when the lady of the house appeared. And she fulfilled her promise. On hands and knees, she scrubbed those stone steps till they shone! The delighted woman paid her a nickel and recommended her services highly. Penny by penny, nickel by nickel, weeks, months later, Marian had enough money. She went back to the pawnshop and bought the violin, certain she was the proud owner of a Stradivarius. A friend of the family taught her how to tune it and play a few notes, but it wasn't long before the strings snapped and the bridge cracked in two. Sitting on the streetcar now, Marian remembered how quickly her career as a violinist had ended.

Later, she'd wheedled her father into buying an old upright piano from his brother. No sooner had the movers placed it in a corner of the Anderson parlor than, giggling with delight, she scrambled onto the bench and ran her fingers up and down the keys, tucking thumb under hand to play a whole octave without stopping, as the pianist at church did. Her family couldn't afford piano lessons, but somehow she acquired a long chart marked with the notes on the staff. Marian propped it behind the keyboard, and picked out the notes one by one until she could accompany herself as she sang simple tunes. For singing was what she liked best. Was she only thirteen when she transferred from the junior to the senior choir? she wondered as the trolley waited for a horse and wagon to clop by. Yes, thirteen—and she'd learned the parts to every piece so she could substitute for anyone who was absent—soprano, alto, tenor, baritone, and bass!

Now she sang for the Y.M.C.A. and other organizations around town. Sometimes she was paid to sing, usually twenty-five or fifty cents, and once in a while a whole dollar!

Nature had blessed Marian with a glorious voice, but to be a good singer, she needed to have voice training. Mr. Robinson, the choirmaster, felt the time had come for her to have voice lessons. He spoke to the congregation about it, and they

11

contributed their pennies and nickels to what they called "The Fund for Marian's Future." Since her father's death a few years ago Marian's mother had worked as a cleaning woman or laundress, and she had all she could do to feed and clothe Marian and her two younger sisters.

The Fund for Marian's Future—my future, she thought, as the streetcar screeched to a stop—today my future is beginning! Making her way through the oncoming rush, she stepped off and checked the address on a slip of paper in her purse. This was it. She looked up at the big gray building squashed between two others. Such a dreary-looking place for a music school! As she entered, the sounds of a piano came floating down the dark stairway and the building was drab no longer. It was the brightest, most cheerful building in Philadelphia! Tucking back a stray lock of hair, Marian took the steps two at a time. _____ SCHOOL OF MUSIC, said the sign on the door. She turned the knob and entered a large reception room filled with chattering girls waiting to fill out application blanks at the registration window. Marian took her place in line. It moved quickly, and when her turn came, she stepped to the window.

"Good morning," she said, smiling at the receptionist, "I would like—"

The receptionist's blue eyes looked past her as if she weren't there. "Would you like an application blank?" she asked the girl behind Marian. Then she called on the next girl . . . and the next.

It must be because I'm younger than the others, Marian reasoned, wondering whether or not to sit down on one of the empty chairs along the wall. She decided she had better stand there. Moving patiently aside, she watched the receptionist answer questions and hand out applications. She was pretty with a cute way of tossing her head so her long curls jounced up and down.

When no one else was left, Marian once again stepped to the window.

12

"What do *you* want?" The receptionist's voice was cool, her upper lip raised, her eyes narrowed to slits. She certainly didn't look pretty now. Marian tried to pay no attention to the coolness in her voice. "I'd like an application blank, please—"

"We don't take colored." BANG . . . the window came down in Marian's face.

Knees shaking, she turned around and walked out. Her thoughts were in a jumble, but more than anything else, she was puzzled. Riding home on the trolley, she wondered how anyone could say such a horrible thing. Across the aisle, a white woman and a Negro woman chatted amiably as they rode together. The Andersons had always lived side by side with white people and Negroes. They helped each other whenever they could. When she and her sisters were small, the Anderson backyard was the meeting place for the neighborhood children. One white girl always stayed later than the others. She had supper with the Andersons, and Mama used to put her to sleep in a big chair until her father came from work to take her home.

Marian had heard there were bigoted people. This was the first time she'd ever met anyone who was rude and unkind to her because her skin was brown. How could anyone as pretty as that receptionist, and lucky enough to be around music all day, be so full of hate?

Glancing out of the trolley window, Marian noticed they were passing the pushcarts on the corner, piled high with everything from big rolls of flypaper to bunches of yellow bananas. Soon she'd be home. What would Mama say? She'd be disappointed, of course, but would she be surprised? Mother had been a schoolteacher in Virginia before she married. Why hadn't she gone back to teaching when Papa died, instead of cleaning people's houses and taking in laundry? Mama had always explained that it took too long to get a teacher's license in Philadelphia. Was that the *only* reason, or wasn't it easy to be a teacher if you were colored?

The motorman called her stop, and Marian got off. She

13

paused a minute to watch some laughing, shouting children, stripped to their underwear, run in and out of the fountain of water that was gushing high from an open hydrant.

A tiny girl about four years old stood on the sidelines. She would step forward as if to join in the fun, but then she'd stop, afraid of the crush of the older children. Suddenly a tall boy boosted her to his shoulders, and waving everyone else out of the way, pranced her into the cooling water. The girl shrieked with delight. She was Negro. The boy was white.

Marian walked the rest of the way slowly. She could never become a real singer if she couldn't take voice lessons. There was that music school, with teachers who could teach her to project her voice, hold a note, and the other things she knew she must learn. Yet, for her it might as well not exist. She turned the corner. She could see Grandmother's house in the middle of a block of row houses. When Father died, Mother couldn't afford to keep their house, so they had moved in with Grandfather and Grandmother Anderson. Grandfather was a gentle man, and Marian and her sisters loved him dearly. Grandmother was a tall, handsome woman, who ruled the household with a firm hand. Aunt Pritchard and her daughters lived there too, and although everyone got along well together, Marian knew that her mother longed for the privacy of her own home again.

Ethel, one of Marian's sisters, sat on the front steps, sucking contentedly on a sliver of ice. "Hi, Marian," she said. "All signed up at school?"

"No." Before Ethel could ask any more questions, Marian hurried into the kitchen to find Mother.

Puffs of steam rose from a huge tub of water bubbling on the black stove. The windows were steamy. The worn linoleum, checkered tablecloth, and the ceiling were covered with moisture. Mama was boiling laundry again.

Marian paused in the doorway and looked at her mother. Mama was so tiny she had to stand on tiptoe to stir the clothes with a piece of old broomstick. Drops of perspiration glistened

14

around her nose. Wisps of hair clung to her forehead. She worked hard, yet never complained.

"Oh, you're back, dear." Mama set down her stick and took off her eyeglasses to wipe away the steam. "When do you start music school?"

"Never." In matter-of-fact tones, Marian told her mother what had happened. "Mama," she asked, "can't I be a singer because I'm colored?"

Mrs. Anderson crossed the kitchen to the brown wooden icebox, opened the door, and took a pitcher of lemonade from the shelf beside a chunk of ice. She set out tall glasses. When she finally spoke, it was calmly, slowly, as if making sure of her words. "Of course you can be a singer, Marian. There will be another way to learn what you need to know."

Marian was not sure. Her stomach quivered when she recalled the look on the receptionist's face. The lemonade tasted sour.

After supper everyone sat out on the front steps to get a breath of air. Usually, Marian would sing a hymn in the evening, and the neighbors would join in, one by one, until the whole street was singing. Tonight, she didn't feel like it. She sat quietly on the bottom step next to Mama.

The door opened, and Aunt Pritchard came out. "You haven't said a word about music school, Marian," she said, fanning herself with a pleated paper fan. "Weren't you going to register today?"

Marian felt Mama nudge her in the side. Mrs. Anderson didn't want Aunt Pritchard to know what had happened at school; Aunty had a temper and was apt to go down there and make a fuss. Mama wouldn't like that. And neither would I, Marian thought.

At that moment, Grandfather was coming around the corner, and she jumped up to greet him. Dressed in his best suit and straw hat, he was coming from synagogue, for Grandfather and Mother weren't Baptists like the other Andersons. Mama was a Methodist, and Grandpa practiced Judaism.

Marian and her sisters thought nothing of the religious differences in the family. Mama had taught them a long time ago that how and where a person worshiped did not matter. "When you come to Him," Mrs. Anderson always said, "He never asks what you are. It's what's in your heart that counts."

Grandfather pinched Marian's cheek. "How's my favorite singer?" he asked.

"Fine." Marian tried to sound cheerful. No point in burdening him with her problem. She wouldn't tell him about music school. "Come on, Grandpa," she said, giving him a hug. "Sit beside me."

It was hot when Marian went to bed, and she couldn't fall asleep. As she lay in the dark bedroom listening to her sisters' quiet breathing, she almost envied them. They didn't have to be concerned about things like music school. Who decided *I* should be the one with the voice? "The Lord," Mama had said, and Marian believed it. But I must have inherited my voice from someone. Mother? Maybe . . . Mama's always singing around the house, and she sang a lot when Papa was alive. Papa! He used to sing too. Marian could almost hear him— his deep voice booming, "Asleep in the Deep" as he dressed to go to work hauling chunks of ice or shoveling coal.

She pictured him tall and straight in the frock coat and top hat he'd worn when he ushered at church. Her throat tightened. How proud he and Mama used to look sitting in the front pew watching her sing! Was her career to be over before it began? When she was younger, she'd thought of becoming a doctor, so she could help people in pain. Maybe she should think about that some more. But music was her life. No matter what, she could not turn her back on it. She plumped up her pillow and asked herself something she had not faced since she left school this afternoon. What would the people at church say? They believed in her. They wanted her to have a music career. It was as if they felt that, because of her voice, she could go to all the places, do all the things, they never could.

16

The darkness started to close in. She saw the girls at the music school in their pretty dresses . . . the receptionist's face with the curled lip, the narrowed eyes . . . then Mama, standing in the middle of the steaming kitchen.

"There will be another way—another way . . ." A cool breeze drifted in through the thin curtains and touched Marian's cheek. Soft darkness surrounded her. She fell into a troubled sleep.

CHAPTER

2

A S D F space semicolon L K J space. A S D F space semi-colon L K J space."

Miss Rogers, Marian's typing teacher, recited the exercise in monotonous rhythm, and the whole class typed in time with her voice.

The room was a clatter of keys, then—*jing*—everyone shifted his carriage in unison. Marian sat at her typewriter, feet planted firmly on the floor, trying to concentrate on striking the right letters. She couldn't keep her mind from wandering. She was to sing at assembly next period, and the notes and words of her music danced around in her head.

Miss Rogers moved up the aisle and looked over Marian's shoulder. "A S D F," she said. Not changing her tone: "Marian Anderson stay after class."

Marian looked at her paper. ZXCV /.,M. She had been typing with her hands on the bottom row instead of the middle! Exasperated, she zipped the paper from the machine and crumpled it into a ball.

The session over, the girls laughed and chattered their way out of the room, but Marian squirmed in her seat waiting for Miss Rogers to speak.

The teacher sat down at her desk and flipped through her rank book until she came to Marian's page. "D . . . F . . . F"—she read aloud. "You failed today's exercise too, Marian. Will you ever learn to concentrate on your typing?"

"I—I hope so, Miss Rogers, but I'm singing at assembly today, and I can't seem to think of anything else."

"I see. Well, go along now, but tomorrow I hope you'll be—" Miss Rogers smiled slightly, "here in mind as well as body."

"Thank you, I'll try." Marian snatched up her books and hurried out of the room, down the corridor toward the auditorium. She'd signed up for the commercial course here at William Penn High, hoping to get a job in an office when she graduated. But no one would want a secretary who was always making mistakes. She ducked into the doorway that led backstage. She would worry about her future later. Now she was going to sing!

"There you are, Marian!" Mr. Morris, the music teacher, hustled her into the wings. Peeking out onto the stage, she saw that Dr. Gray, the principal, was announcing her selection. She patted her hair into place and straightened her plaid skirt. Pulling back her shoulders, she walked onstage. The auditorium was jam-packed with students, teachers, and guests, but Marian wasn't nervous. Audiences didn't make her nearly as jumpy as typewriters!

Sitting down at the piano, she played and sang one of the spirituals she'd learned at church, "He's Got the Whole World in His Hands." Everyone was moved by the richness of her voice and the sincere way she sang the words.

When she finished, there was loud applause. Bowing, she went backstage to pick up her books.

"Marian," someone called, "Dr. Gray wants to see you."

Oh dear, she thought, crossing the hall, Miss Rogers must have told him about my typing. The principal's door was open; he sat behind his desk, deep in conversation with a tall man she'd never seen before.

"Excuse me—"

"Come in, come in, Marian. This is Dr. Roher from the School Department. He just heard you sing—"

Dr. Roher turned to face her. "Yes, young lady, and I don't

19

understand why you're taking commercial subjects. You should be in a straight college course studying as much music as possible."

"Thank you, sir. But I can't afford to go to college. I have to get a job when I graduate."

"Just the same, I think you should transfer to South Philadelphia High, where the course of studies will be more suitable. You can't fit a square peg into a round hole, you know!"

Marian was more confused than ever. Even if she took every music class the high school had to offer, it wouldn't be enough. If singing were to be her career, she had to be trained by a professional voice teacher. If she couldn't go to music school because she was colored, and she couldn't study typing and shorthand and get a job, how was she ever going to make enough money so Mama could stop working?

"There will be another way to learn what you need to know," Mama said whenever Marian mentioned singing lessons. She certainly hoped it would come along soon.

That afternoon Marian went to choir practice right from school. As she climbed the back steps to the choir loft, she heard the murmur of men talking. She recognized their voices: Mr. Robinson, the choirmaster, and the Reverend Mr. Parks, the pastor.

"Of course we must have Roland Hayes for the Gala Concert again this year," the Reverend Mr. Parks was saying. "He has a magnificent voice, and we're all proud of him. But the last time he was here, he sang some of his songs in foreign languages, and most of our congregation didn't understand the words. Let's have Marian sing a few songs on the program too. *Everyone* understands *her!*"

Marian ran up the rest of the steps. "*Me* sing with Roland Hayes?" she cried, bursting into the room. "Do you mean it?"

"Oh, Marian, you heard!" Mr. Robinson's eyes twinkled. "Yes, we'll have to speak to Mr. Hayes about it, but I'm sure it'll be all right with him."

Marian trembled. She, Marian Anderson, singing on the

20

same platform as the great Roland Hayes! Hayes sang spirituals, the beautiful songs made up by Negroes in slavery, expressing their misery, their protest. Hayes was also the first American Negro with enough musical background to sing serious classical music like Schubert, Handel, Brahms, and arias from famous operas.

From whom did Mr. Hayes take lessons? she wondered, as she walked home through the darkening streets, her sweater buttoned high against the autumn chill. Mr. Hayes was a Negro, and he'd become a great singer. Maybe there was a way for her too. Maybe Mama was right.

Rounding the corner, Marian ran up the block and bounded into the house, eager to tell her mother everything that happened. "Mama!" she called. "I'm home!" She stopped short. Strains of music came drifting from the parlor. Grandmother was seated at the organ, her body moving from side to side as her feet pumped the pedals. "Your mother's working late," she said, without stopping her playing. "Supper's on the stove."

"Oh." Marian was disappointed. She had to tell someone the good news. "Grandma," she blurted, "Roland Hayes is coming to sing in the Gala Concert again, and this time I'm going to sing in it too!" She hesitated. More words came tumbling out. "Maybe I'll ask *him* about singing lessons—" She clapped her hand over her mouth. She hadn't meant to say anything about that.

Grandmother's body stopped swaying. Lifting her hands from the keyboard, she turned to face her granddaughter squarely. As she'd said dozens of times before: "You know how to sing, Marian. Why do you need lessons?"

"Because—oh, never mind." Marian stomped out to the kitchen. She loved her Grandmother, but she simply didn't understand!

The following Sunday, Mama came to the Baptist Church to hear Marian sing. When the service was over, the collection box was passed. As Marian and Mama left the church, the

Reverend Mr. Parks tucked some money, seventeen dollars and two cents, into Mrs. Anderson's coat pocket. "To buy our Marian a new dress for the Gala Concert," he said.

"How'd they know I needed a new dress?" Marian whispered as she and Mama made their way down the church steps, nodding and smiling at their friends and neighbors.

"Oh, I guess they want you to look nice." Mrs. Anderson beamed with pride. "It isn't every girl who can sing on the same program as Roland Hayes!"

And while Marian and her mother walked home through the streets of South Philadelphia that quiet Sunday morning, Marian Anderson vowed to do her best to bring honor to the good people who had always been so kind to her.

The next few weeks were hectic. Marian went shopping and found that the dress she wanted was too expensive. Instead, she bought a length of white satin and some gold braid trimmed with tiny leaves. With Mother's help, she set about making the dress herself.

Gradually Marian was getting settled in the new high school, singing for Y.M.C.A.'s and other organizations in the evening, rehearsing for the Gala Concert, and working on her dress in her "spare time."

On the day of the concert, Marian, along with the rest of the congregation, was enthralled, as Roland Hayes, tears streaming down his cheeks, sang the spirituals of his people. The depth of feeling in his tenor voice, his genius, his artistry, seemed to cast the songs in silver and gold. No one could ever have sung spirituals so well. She was entranced, too, by his French, Italian, and German selections. Though she understood few of the words, the melodies were lovely. If she were to be a true artist, she must also learn this kind of music.

The concert over, everyone crowded around, eager to congratulate Mr. Hayes and shake the famous singer's hand. In the confusion, Marian didn't get a chance to ask him about lessons, but that evening, to her delight, he paid the Andersons a visit.

"Marian has a lovely voice," he said to Mother and Grandmother, as they sat together in the parlor. "After I heard her sing last time I was here, I told my singing teacher in Boston about her." Mr. Hayes paused, and looked at Mother and Grandmother. "Mr. Hubbard has agreed to take Marian on as a pupil," he finished, glancing at her from the corner of his eye.

Marian caught her breath and started to say something, but Grandmother spoke first. "We thank you kindly for your interest, Mr. Hayes, but we couldn't possibly afford the expense."

"I understand that, Mrs. Anderson, but Mr. Hubbard has agreed to let Marian earn her own way by helping his wife around the house."

"No." Grandmother shook her head vigorously. "I do not approve of a young girl leaving home."

From tenor, Roland Hayes, came the inspiration for a career in music.

Marian leaned forward. "But, Grandmother—"

Mama placed her finger over her lips in a signal to be quiet. No one argued with Grandmother. The subject was closed. Marian did not go.

She continued to sing for various organizations throughout Philadelphia, and little by little, her popularity increased. Sometimes, she was rushing about from one place to another, making two or three appearances in one night. After a while, she was earning as much as five dollars a performance! From this, she always gave her sisters Alyce and Ethel a dollar each, kept a dollar for herself, and gave the remaining two dollars to her mother. The money was a great help, but Marian never sang for money alone. She sang because she wanted to bring the beauty of music to others.

She joined the Philadelphia Choral Society, a Negro group that sang for the sheer joy of it. Once, one of the leaders of the group, a Mr. Young, came to see Mother. "Mrs. Anderson," he said solemnly, "someday that child will sing for fifty dollars a night." His voice deepened. "Mark my words," he said, "fifty dollars a night!" To Marian that seemed incredible.

Then something happened that made her think perhaps there *was* a chance to make singing her career. When she was a junior in high school, she met Mary Patterson, a Negro singer who lived nearby and had studied uptown with a vocal teacher. Mrs. Patterson listened to Marian sing and offered to give her lessons without charge.

Singing lessons at last! Marian was thrilled. Mrs. Patterson taught her to use her voice without straining it, to direct it toward a corner of the ceiling, and how to sing a few German songs. Mrs. Patterson was kind in other ways too. When Marian needed an evening gown to wear for her public appearances, the teacher gave her one of her own to make over. Marian liked Mrs. Patterson's gown so much she wore it for years, and saved the pieces as a remembrance.

Mrs. Patterson, however, was a soprano. When Marian had

studied with her a few months, the teacher suggested her pupil make a change. "Marian, I've taught you all I can," she said. "Now you should be studying uptown with Agnes Reifsnyder. She's a contralto like you, and she can help you with your low tones."

Marian had become fond of Mrs. Patterson and she hated to leave her. But she knew that if singing were to be her career, she must progress. Once again, her friends and neighbors rallied around. The Philadelphia Choral Society held a benefit concert to raise funds for Marian's lessons with Mrs. Reifsnyder. The soloist at the concert? Marian Anderson herself!

Shortly before Marian's graduation from high school, Dr. Lucy Wilson, her principal, arranged for her to meet Giuseppe Boghetti, a well-known vocal coach who had trained many famous concert singers and opera stars. Making an appointment with "the great Boghetti" was difficult, but fortunately, Dr. Wilson knew Lisa Roma, one of Boghetti's pupils, and after hearing Marian sing, Miss Roma arranged the audition.

Marian's knees shook as she stood outside the door of Boghetti's studio, with Dr. Wilson on one side of her, Lisa Roma on the other.

The door opened. A short man with rumpled black hair stood in the doorway. He looked at Dr. Wilson, at Lisa Roma, then at Marian. "I am tired," he said. "I have more pupils than I need already. Make no mistake. I listen to you only as a favor to Miss Roma. Understand?"

Marian nodded and handed him her music.

"Deep River," he said, glancing at it as they stepped inside. "I never heard it. All right—" He sat down at the baby grand piano near the window and played the introduction.

Marian closed her eyes and sang:

> "Deep River, my home is over Jordan,
> Deep River, Lord, I want to cross
>   over into campground.
> Oh, don't you want to go to the gospel feast

That promised land, where all is peace?
Oh, Deep River, Lord, Deep River."

Marian sang the words from her heart. They touched her
deeply, perhaps because rivers have a special meaning for her
race. Before the War Between the States, to cross a river into
a northern state often meant freedom from slavery.

When she had finished, she looked out of the window, up
at the ceiling—anywhere but at Boghetti's face. The room
was still except for the snap of Dr. Wilson's purse as she
reached for a handkerchief.

Boghetti cleared his throat. "Please," he said, handing
Marian a scale, "sing this."

Trying to keep her voice from trembling, Marian did as he
asked.

Boghetti said, "I will make room for you at once. I will need
only two years with you. After that, you will be able to go
anywhere, sing for anybody."

Go anywhere! Sing for anybody! Marian felt light-headed.
Boghetti started to talk about his fee, and her heart sank. She
couldn't possibly afford it. She was earning more money by
singing than she ever had. Mama was a cleaning woman in a
department store now, but she looked so worn and thin that
Marian wanted her to leave. With Ethel and Alyce in high
school, expenses were higher than ever. They seemed to be
needing something every day—shoes, or gym suits, or books.
Boghetti's fee would not fit into the budget. But how to ex-
plain all this? Instead, Marian murmured, "Thank you, sir, for
listening to me. But I'm afraid I can't afford—"

"We shall see what can be done," said Dr. Wilson. Before
Marian could protest, the principal hustled her out of the
door.

Once again, Marian's good friends came to her aid. Dr.
Wilson told them about Boghetti, and they arranged another
concert at church with Roland Hayes as one of the soloists.
So many people attended that the concert raised over six hun-

26

dred dollars, and Marian started her studies with Giuseppe Boghetti immediately.

Years later Boghetti described his first impression of her. "When she finished singing 'Deep River,' I just couldn't move," he said. "She had none of the refinements. She simply sang it the way she felt it, with all her natural feeling for music."

Boghetti was a perfectionist, and when he discovered uneven tones in Marian's scale, he set to work at once to even them out. First, he had her hum a tune until she could feel the vibration. Then he had her place the tone exactly where she'd been humming. He was determined that she develop an even, unbroken vocal line from her lowest tone to her highest.

He taught her to breathe correctly. Until now, Marian had paid little attention to how she breathed when she sang. Boghetti suggested that she hold her hands against her ribs, breathe slowly, and see how far apart she could expand her rib cage. Eventually, he explained, by exercising the abdominal muscles, she would be able to expand them farther. This would mean more breath, greater vocal power.

"Nature has given you a voice," he said, "but there is no shortcut to becoming a real professional. Only when you understand the *how* and *why* of singing will you be able to perform well no matter how you feel."

Boghetti was a hard taskmaster. He had neither time nor patience for anyone who did not practice. "If you don't study," he'd tell his pupils, "I don't want you. I don't take 'society people' who think it would 'be nice' to sing."

Finding time to practice was not easy for Marian. To graduate from high school she had to keep up with her studies, and she was singing in public more often than ever. To make matters worse, it seemed as if whenever she did try to sing at home, her sisters or cousins were studying, and couldn't be disturbed. She did the best she could. The night before her lessons she took her music to bed with her and studied silently until she could stay awake no longer. She looked at her music

27

in school, between classes and at lunchtime. One way or another, she usually had it memorized by the time she arrived at Boghetti's studio.

"Ah, I see you have studied well this week," he'd say.

Marian would nod, but she felt she wasn't spending nearly enough time actually singing. If only she and her mother and sisters could have a small house of their own, with an extra room where she could sing without disturbing anyone. Someday, perhaps . . .

Though she didn't feel she was getting enough practice, studying with Boghetti was stimulating. He taught her classical songs and arias from operas like those Roland Hayes sang. Sometimes she and Boghetti acted out whole operatic scenes together. Marian liked opera and acting. She often went to plays presented by a group of talented Negro actors, and she thought of making opera her career.

Boghetti discouraged her. "For you," he said, "the concert stage is better."

Marian knew why. In America, Negroes were not welcome in opera. In fact no Negro, not even Roland Hayes, had ever been invited to sing with the Metropolitan Opera Company. She could not understand what the color of a person's skin had to do with the sound of his voice.

3

THE flurry of high school graduation was over, and with schoolwork off her mind, Marian could accept more singing engagements. She began to think of teaming up with a pianist, for although she had taken lessons and accompanied herself quite well, she knew that a good accompanist would enhance her voice and leave her free to concentrate on singing.

One night she was on a whirlwind, appearing in three different places in the same evening, and she arrived at the Y.M.C.A. breathless from the rush. After taking a few minutes to catch her breath, she sat down at the piano, opened her music, and played and sang her first selection. She bowed her head waiting for the applause to die down. When she looked up, a tall young man was standing beside her, Billy King, one of the best accompanists in Philadelphia. He often played for great artists when they came to town. Marian was sure he would not want to accompany her.

She was wrong. Billy leaned over and whispered: "May I have the honor of playing your next number?"

Marian nodded. She was so excited she didn't think she could sing, but with King at the piano, her voice sounded better than ever.

Marian didn't team up with King at once, however. He was working as regular accompanist for an older, more experienced singer, Lydia McLain. Sometimes Lydia and Marian were asked to sing on the same program, so occasionally King played for Marian as well. He was a good musician with a keen sense of rhythm, and his playing blended well with her voice.

That winter Marian and Lydia were both asked to sing at a church in Orange, New Jersey. They took the train together along with Billy and a tall, handsome doctor friend of Lydia's.

"Are you going to Orange to see a patient, Doctor?" Billy asked, as the four young people settled down in their seats.

"No—" And the doctor and Lydia glanced at each other and smiled.

He's probably going to hear Lydia sing, Marian thought. She took some music from her black music case and started to discuss it with Billy.

The trip went quickly, and before long the conductor called, "Orange . . . Orange, New Jersey."

Marian tucked the music back in her case, and she and Billy got up to leave. Lydia and the doctor stayed in their seats, looking at a big map they had spread across their laps.

"Hurry, Lydia—" But the conductor hustled Marian and Billy down the aisle and off the train. No sooner had they set foot on the crowded platform than the whistle blew and the train moved on.

"Lydia!" Marian gasped. "The concert!"

"Maybe they're going to visit some friends in Passaic," said Billy. "They'll probably meet us at the church later."

"Odd they didn't mention it." Marian glanced at her watch. "Well," she shrugged, "there's plenty of time. It's only five, and the concert doesn't start till eight thirty."

Eight thirty came and no Lydia.

The chairman of the program committee demanded to know where she was.

"I'm sure she'll be here any minute," said Billy.

"We'll wait half an hour longer. If she's not here by then, you'll have to go on without her."

Nine o'clock and no Lydia, so with Billy at the piano, Marian sang the whole program herself. The next day they found out that Lydia and her tall, handsome young doctor friend had run off to New York City to get married!

Billy became Marian's regular accompanist, and later her manager as well. His energy and efficiency helped her career enormously. He had accompanied famous artists in many different cities, and he wrote dozens of letters telling of his new singer. He was choirmaster and organist at an Episcopal church in Philadelphia, and when out-of-town guests visited his church, he often persuaded them to set up singing dates for organizations in their home cities. He prepared pamphlets and flyers, billing her as Marian E. Anderson. The "E.," he explained, was something extra, like a "grace note."

Billy came to Marian's house to meet her family and took her home to meet his parents. His house was a "row house" like Grandmother's, but detached on one side, so he and Marian could practice there without disturbing the neighbors.

One day they were in Billy's living room practicing, and his mother was in the kitchen, listening. "Billy," she called out when they had finished. "You'd better study if you don't want Marian to leave you behind. Her voice sounds more beautiful every day!"

One engagement led to another, and gradually Marian's fees grew higher, until she sometimes earned the fifty dollars a night Mr. Young of the Choral Society had predicted. Eventually, she passed the fifty-dollar mark and started to earn as much as a hundred dollars a night. With Billy at the piano, she appeared at churches, in theaters, schools, halls, clubs, and at parties in private homes. Often she and Billy were invited to perform at Negro schools in the South, from big colleges like Hampton Institute and Howard University, down to one-room schoolhouses in the backwoods, where they accepted a small fee or none at all.

One evening, she and Billy were in Virginia performing at Hampton. The great Negro musician and composer, R. Nathanial Dett, who led the famous Hampton Choir, took Marian for a drive, and they talked of her future in music. "You should not compromise," he said. "You'll have many sacrifices to make, but even if your dreams never come true, the effort in itself is worthwhile."

Marian had heard of the segregation laws in the South. She had encountered them for the first time while she was in high school on her way to sing in Savannah, Georgia. Her mother had accompanied her, and when they changed trains in Washington, D.C., they were obliged to ride in the car "For Negroes Only." It was hot, stuffy, and dirty, but that didn't bother Marian nearly as much as the expressions on the faces of some of her fellow passengers. They looked discouraged, humiliated, as if they were being stepped on.

Not Marian. No matter how many times she was offended for the fact she was a Negro, Marian Anderson rose above ignorance. She held her head high, wore her color proudly.

It was on a train with Billy that she met segregation for the second time. They were traveling in the South one afternoon to perform in an evening concert, when a porter came walking up the aisle.

"May I speak with you?" Billy asked in a low voice.

The porter paused.

"I'm Billy King and this is Marian Anderson, the singer. We're on our way to appear in a concert. Is there any chance of our getting a hot dinner?"

The porter beamed. "Glad to meet you!" he said, shaking their hands vigorously. "You played at our church last month. You were grand! Wait here now—I'll be right back." The porter hurried on through the coach and returned a few minutes later. "Come into the dining car at five," he whispered breathlessly.

At five of five, Billy and Marian got up from their seats and started toward the rear of the train. Passing through a coach reserved "For White People Only," Marian could not help noticing how much cleaner and more comfortable it was than the one for Negroes. They paused as they entered the dining car. It was early for dinner and no one was sitting at the tables.

The car was empty except for a headwaiter in a white jacket.

"Good evening, Miss Anderson—Mr. King," he said cordially. "Will you step this way?"

Marian and Billy followed him to the far end of the car.

"Right here, please." He motioned toward a table with an open curtain hanging in front.

Obviously, it was the waiters' table. The curtain could be drawn in case anyone came in before they finished. But Marian smiled as the headwaiter pulled out her chair. It wasn't his fault. He did his best to make them comfortable. He seemed delighted they had come.

As she became more well known, arrangements could sometimes be made for Marian to travel in a special private room if it hadn't already been sold. She traveled by auto whenever possible. She wanted no particular favors, and would have been as happy to travel in the Negro coach. But unless she had a comfortable trip, she was apt to arrive at a concert tired, unable to give her top performance, and to Marian, singing her best was what mattered most.

Back in Philadelphia, Marian and Billy were scheduled to appear in a program along with Madame _____, a famous singer from the Midwest. They'd been booked, because Philadelphia was Marian's hometown, and the concert manager figured that many of her friends would attend.

As usual Marian and Billy took the streetcar to the concert hall, where Billy would accompany both singers. They got out in front of the hall as a long black automobile pulled up, driven by a chauffeur so smartly uniformed that Marian wasn't surprised when he clicked his heels and bowed as he opened the back door for his passenger. Out she stepped, a short, plump figure. Madame _____ was resplendent in a green satin evening gown with a train so long, the chauffeur carried it gallantly above the ground, as its proud owner swept across the sidewalk and sailed through the stage door.

Marian glanced down at her own dress, the same simple gray one Mrs. Patterson had given her.

33

Marian and Billy entered the hall, and the sound of a woman's voice rose above the backstage hustle and bustle. It was Madame. She was waving a printed program in the concert manager's face. "Marian Anderson," she shrieked, "who is she?" And without waiting for an answer: "How dare you engage an unknown to sing on the same program with me?"

"But, Madame, Miss Anderson's singing only two songs—" The concert manager backed into a corner.

"H'mmm—" Madame held the program to the light. "When?" she asked, squinting up at it. "This—this printing's too small."

"One at the end of the first half; one at the end of the second."

"You mean *she* sings after *me?*" Yellow feathers quivered atop Madame's upswept coiffure. "Impossible! The audience should be left with the sound of *my* voice in their ears—not some—some unknown's!"

The concert manager looked up and saw Marian and Billy standing there. "P—please, Madame—here is Miss Anderson—"

Madame turned around. "Well!" she exclaimed. She flounced off to her dressing room, her chauffeur in her wake.

Marian found herself a quiet corner, had a cup of tea, and looked over her music. She was determined not to let anything upset her performance.

The program started, and with Billy at the piano Madame sang four songs. The audience applauded politely, and Madame bowed and left the stage.

Then Marian sang one number. The audience clapped, cheered. "Bravo!" they called. "Encore!"

But Marian didn't wish to offend Madame any further, so without singing an encore she retired backstage. The concert manager was cornered again, Madame's plump finger waggling in his face. She was insisting that he announce to the audience that she was singing under the handicap of a "severe case of laryngitis."

34

Only after the announcement was made did Madame sing her last four songs. The applause this time was a bit stronger —in tribute, evidently, to her courage in performing "under stress."

Madame bowed and waited. Calls for encore not forth-coming, she turned to make her exit, Billy slightly behind.

Suddenly, a sickening R-R-I-P! The audience let out a roar. Billy had stepped on Madame's train! The shiny green stream, spread across the floor of the stage, was marred by his foot-print. He followed a flustered Madame into the wings.

"I'm sorry, Madame—"

"Sorry?" Madame's eye bulged unflatteringly. "You did it on purpose. You—you—"

The concert manager hustled her out of the door.

Marian tried not to laugh. "Billy, did you—"

He held up his hand with mock solemnity. "I give you my word, Marian, it was an accident." His face relaxed in a grin. "That is, I think it was. Sh-h-h, we're on now."

Marian and Billy entered the stage. When the audience finally quieted down, they started their next number.

Marian was not even twenty when she felt she was earning enough money to make one of her fondest dreams come true— to buy Mother a home of her own. When the family across the street from Grandmother's put their frame house up for sale, she went to see it at once. The house seemed made for them. It had two bedrooms, one for Marian and her mother, one for her sisters. There was enough land in back to add a first-floor bathroom so that the one upstairs could be made into a small studio.

Grandmother was against the whole idea. "It's too risky for you to buy a house," she said. "Why, you're barely out of high school, Marian. What if you can't keep up the payments?"

This time Grandmother did not get her way. The down payment was made, the deed signed, and a few days later Marian and her sister Ethel went shopping for furniture. They selected an overstuffed sofa and two chairs, and Marian asked the salesman to make arrangements for payments on the installment plan.

"Who's responsible for the payments?" he asked.

"I am," replied Marian.

"But you're so young—"

"I can handle them." Marian looked the salesman straight in the eye, trying to sound more confident than she felt. Perhaps Grandmother was right. Singing was not the most stable way of making a living.

Suddenly music came floating in from another part of the store. Marian tilted her head and listened. Someone was singing "Deep River," and whoever it was sounded very familiar!

"It's you, Marian!" Ethel exclaimed. "I didn't know your record was out yet!"

"Neither did I. I made it just a few weeks ago."

The salesman's eyes widened. "That's your voice?" he asked.

Marian nodded. She was so numb with embarrassment, she couldn't say a word.

The salesman sank down in a big chair and listened to the record until it was finished. He reached for his order book. "With a voice like that," he said, "you should have no trouble making the payments. Name and address, please?"

"Marian Anderson. South Martin Street."

"South Martin Street," he repeated, writing it down. "Well, Miss Marian Anderson, if I don't miss my guess, someday you'll have your whole family living on *Easy Street!*"

The house became a real home, and as Marian traveled about on one concert tour after another, riding in trains, living in cold hotel rooms, she always looked forward to returning to the house in Philadelphia, filled with laughter, and music, and love.

She was home between tours one day, busy at her sewing machine, when the doorbell rang.

"Marian, come on down here. There's a Mr. Fisher waiting

36

to see you," Alyce called upstairs to announce the visitor.

"Fisher? I don't know anyone by that name." Finally she remembered. There, standing in the doorway was Leon Fisher, a young chemist she had met the last time she sang in Wilmington.

"Hello," she said, trying not to look surprised. "Won't you come in?"

They chatted a few minutes, and then he left to return an hour later with his brother Orpheus, nicknamed King. King was studying to be an architect and attended art school in Philadelphia. After that he came to visit Marian whenever she was home. They enjoyed many of the same things and continued to see each other until he finished art school and went to New York to study. Marian knew she would miss him. She cried when he left. But then she got caught up in her own busy life again, singing in concerts and traveling almost constantly.

King wrote her often. In one of his letters he said he thought it was high time they sent their clothes to the laundry in the same bundle. This was his way of asking her to be his wife. She liked him enormously, and perhaps loved him. But marriage now, she felt, would interfere with her career and would not be fair to either of them.

What was it Mr. Dett had said about the sacrifices she'd have to make for her career? Perhaps she had just made the biggest sacrifice of all.

CHAPTER

4

I WILL need only two years with you," Boghetti had said
the first time he heard Marian sing. "Then you will be
able to go anywhere, sing for anybody!"

The two years had passed. With Boghetti as her teacher,
she had become more sure of herself. Her voice had matured.
She felt it was beginning to "speak in a new way," as she put
it. Still, she had a long road to travel to become a "concert
artist" rather than a "recital singer."

After a sellout performance in Harlem one night, the young
concert manager or impresario who sponsored her there offered to arrange a recital at New York's Town Hall.

This might be her big chance! A successful recital at Town
Hall, with good reviews in the New York papers, and she
would be asked to sing for large audiences in the finest halls
in the country. Her fees would increase. She would "have
arrived." Business arrangements for such a recital weren't anything like those for her regular engagements, however. She
would not be paid, and would have to pay the expenses herself. If too few tickets were sold, her savings would go for
nothing. Usually a talented young singer had a socially-
prominent "patron of the arts" to pay for her debut, but not
Marian. "She sings beautifully," many society people said,
"but, after all, she's a Negro."

This didn't surprise her. She knew, she had known since
that day she'd been turned down at music school, that reach-

ing the top would be twice as hard for her as for a white person. She refused to feel bitter about it. "The Lord isn't prejudiced," she said. "He gave this gift to a Negro."

She asked Mr. Boghetti if he thought she was ready for Town Hall. If he had any doubts, he didn't mention them. And one night when she and her family were sitting in the parlor of their home, she asked them what they thought.

Ethel, eighteen now, was in her favorite position, curled up on the living room floor, gazing at the artificial flames in the fireplace. "Why shouldn't you be ready?" she asked. "Who else sings as well as you?"

"Well, there's always Galli-Curci and Schumann-Heink," said Alyce, motioning toward a stack of records on the phonograph.

Marian smiled and turned to her mother. "Seriously, Mama, do you think I'm ready?"

"To us your voice always sounds wonderful, dear. But you must make up your own mind."

"What if I can't?"

"Then pray for the Lord to help you."

Marian did pray. And she tried to think out the problem from every angle. First of all, she had just turned twenty, and most singers waited until their late twenties or thirties to be presented at a place like Town Hall. On the other hand, most singers didn't start singing in public as young as she. Besides, the newspapers had been taking lots more notice of her lately. At first, only Negro papers had printed articles about her, but now critics on white papers came to hear her sing, and often gave her fine reviews. She had appeared in dozens of small concert halls and theaters throughout the East, and had sung in New York several times, in churches, at a big Baptist convention, at a concert for the National Association for the Advancement of Colored People.

As for risking her savings, perhaps that was another of the sacrifices Mr. Dett had mentioned. She told the young impresario to go ahead with arrangements for Town Hall and spent the next few months preparing her program. She decided she would not limit it to Negro spirituals. Above all, she wanted to be judged, not as a Negro singer, but as a singer who happened to be a Negro. She worked hard, learning classical pieces in French, Italian, and German, like those Roland Hayes sang. She did not understand the languages, but her high school French helped a little. Boghetti coached her in Italian, and she learned the German words phonetically, sound by sound. Singing in German was especially difficult, because it had so many guttural sounds. She practiced them over and over again, and Boghetti seemed satisfied.

The day of the recital dawned dark and gray, a fine April mist falling from heavy clouds. Marian followed Boghetti's instructions to the letter, an early train from Philadelphia to New York, a cab to the Y.W.C.A. in Harlem, where she was staying because Manhattan hotels wouldn't admit Negroes, a light supper at four, a rest, and then to the hall to practice her vocal exercises. She was excited, but she had no qualms.

Billy arrived at the hall at eight, half an hour before curtain time. "Are the tickets selling well?" he asked the impresario.

"Yes, we'll have a full house." The impresario hurried away.

At eight fifteen, Marian and Billy sat down in the artists' room and sipped a cup of tea. They waited for the signal to go onstage. Eight thirty . . . No one came to get them.

"What do you suppose is wrong?" Marian asked.

"Oh, probably a minor delay," said Billy.

It was nine o'clock before the impresario reappeared. "You may as well begin," he said, shrugging his shoulders.

May as well? What did he mean by that? There wasn't time to ask. The performance was half an hour late already. Taking Billy's hand, Marian walked onstage and gazed out over the hall. It was almost empty! Only a few people sat in the front section, a few more in the center and back, and up in the balcony, practically no one. Row after row of empty

40

seats. The concert manager had said tickets were selling well, that they'd have a full house! It dawned on her: he'd said that so she wouldn't get nervous. That's why he'd delayed the curtain, hoping more people would come. She felt weak, as if her enthusiasm, her joy in singing, were being wrung out of her like water from wet clothes.

Bowing to the meager audience, she forced herself to smile. She was thankful that Billy was here. At least she didn't have to face them alone. She looked back at the piano and nodded for him to begin. The piano bench was empty. Where was he?

"Psst, over here, Marian."

In the disappointment of singing to a nearly empty house, she had almost forgotten that Billy was to accompany her first number at the organ instead of the piano. He was seated across the stage, and she had never felt so alone in her life!

The deep, rich chords of the organ rang through the auditorium. Marian closed her eyes and lifted her voice. The audience, what there was of it, clapped after each number. The empty hall, however, seemed to echo their applause in hollow mockery. Usually, time flew when she sang. Tonight it dragged, and she felt as if the program would never end. When it was over at last, she tried to judge her performance: Not too bad, except for my Brahms. Roland Hayes sings Brahms with much more feeling.

Back at the Y, she slept restlessly, and when morning crept into the room, she was bone-tired. She dressed quickly and went downstairs for the newspaper. She turned to the music section. The review was at the bottom of the page.

> Marian Anderson sang her
> Brahms as if by rote . . .

"By rote . . . ," from memory alone, without feeling.

The reviewer was right. Boghetti's words buzzed in her head. *When you understand the how and why, you'll perform well no matter how you feel.* Obviously she didn't understand the *how* and the *why*. She had failed. She had been foolish,

41

brash, trying to make her debut in one of the finest concert halls in the country before she was ready. She had let everyone down—Boghetti, her family, Billy, the people at church.

It was over. She never wanted to see, or hear, or sing another note of music as long as she lived.

When she returned to Philadelphia, she felt miserable. Awake or asleep, she relived that evening over and over again. She blamed no one but herself. She'd been too impatient. She should have waited.

Mother was calm. "Listen, my child," she said, "whatever you do in this world—no matter how good it is—you'll never please everyone. You can only do your best."

"No, Mother. I'd better forget about singing and do something else. Remember when I used to think about becoming a doctor? Maybe I'll—"

"Well, why don't you think about it a little and pray a lot first?" said Mama.

Even her mother's wise counsel couldn't help Marian. She locked herself in her upstairs studio and refused to see anyone for days, weeks, months; not even Billy or Mr. Boghetti. She couldn't bring herself to sing a note. The house, once so full of joy and music, was gloomy and silent.

One night Mother came home from work especially weary. Marian wasn't surprised. Once in a while when she and her sisters were in school, they used to stop by at the department store where Mama worked, and she was always working twice as hard as anyone else. It was obvious that her supervisor took advantage of Mama's uncomplaining nature by giving her chores no one else wanted. Tonight her eyes looked dull, the lines in her forehead deeper than ever. Marian called Dr. Taylor, who lived nearby, and asked him to come at once.

"She must stay home a few days," Dr. Taylor said after making his examination. "She's not well enough to work."

Next morning Mama was up and dressed at her usual time. She was going despite doctor's orders. Marian knew why. The payment on the house was due.

"Go back to bed, Mama," she ordered. Picking up the phone, she called the department store. "This is Marian Anderson," she said to the supervisor. "I want to tell you my mother won't be coming in today." She paused, "Not today or ever again."

"Marian!" Mama gasped. "What have you done?"

"What I've wanted to do for years. Go back to bed, Mama." Marian hung up and called another number. "Billy? This is Marian. I'm ready to go back to work."

"Good." Billy did not sound surprised. "I'll set up some engagements."

As Marian turned away from the phone, a wave of happiness surged through her. She pressed her lips together and started to hum for the first time in almost a year!

"My prayers have been answered," Mama called from her bed.

"Perhaps mine have too." Marian went to her mother's room, leaned over her, and kissed her forehead. "Now rest, Mama," she said softly. "I have work to do." She hurried to her studio, pulled her music from a bottom drawer, sat down at the piano, and started to sing.

After a few days' rest, Mrs. Anderson was well, but Marian never allowed her to work again. Now the house became even more of a home with Mama bustling about the tidy kitchen, cooking her daughters' favorite dishes, always ready to listen to their problems and give quiet counsel.

Marian took up her career where she'd left off, with a greater will than before. She went to Boghetti's studio more often, determined to give her voice the polish it needed. She studied French with a local high school teacher and concentrated harder on Italian with Boghetti. German, however, was still an enigma. She couldn't find a German teacher, so whenever she learned a German song she tried to sing it for someone who spoke the language and could help her with the meaning and pronunciation of the words. She knew that wasn't enough. Town Hall had taught her that she couldn't pretend a storehouse of knowledge by collecting a little. To sing German well she had to learn the language fluently. How? When?

Meantime, she and Billy started their tours again, and before long Marian was earning enough money to take care of her family and start another savings account. Her fees remained the same. She was a "recital singer," not a "concert artist," but her hopes and ambitions, her determination to get to the top, had returned. Marian Anderson had stumbled. Now she was back on her feet.

CHAPTER

5

IT WAS a hot summer day a few months after Marian had
gone back to work. She and Mr. Boghetti were in Aoelian
Hall in New York awaiting her turn to try out in the preliminaries of a big singing contest. She had lost some of her
self-confidence since her failure at Town Hall. Her stomach
quivered as she looked around the auditorium packed with
three hundred singers from all over the country competing
for first prize, a chance to sing with the New York Philharmonic at Lewisohn Stadium, New York's great outdoor singing arena.

"Don't worry," said Boghetti. "You'll do fine."

She sat back and tried to relax. This wasn't her first com-
petition. She had won a contest sponsored by the Philadelphia
Philharmonic, but for some reason it hadn't made any notice-
able difference in her career. She was at a standstill, and her
engagements were much the same as before, in churches, for
organizations, in schools and private homes. This contest
was another matter. Winning would surely be a step upward.
Winning? How could she think of winning? These were only
the preliminaries.

A voice came over the loudspeaker:

"EACH CONTESTANT IS TO COME TO THE STAGE
WHEN HIS NUMBER IS CALLED, START SINGING,
AND STOP IMMEDIATELY IF THE GONG RINGS."

The parade of contestants began—sopranos, altos, contraltos. Some were good, some not so good, and many were gonged out after a few bars.

"The judges must be in a hurry to go home," said Boghetti, wiping the perspiration from his forehead. "It's so hot, I don't blame them." His voice dropped to a whisper. "But you, Marian, are to continue singing even if the gong rings. Understand? I want them to hear your trill at the end."

Marian nodded, but she doubted if she could do it. Was Boghetti afraid she'd be eliminated quickly because she was Negro?

"Remember what I told you," he whispered, as she got up. "Walk to the stage slowly—don't waste breath. And don't stop singing until the end. Good luck!"

He needn't have told her to walk slowly. Her knees were shaking hard. But the expression on her face remained calm. Head high, she climbed the steps to the stage, closed her eyes, and started to sing, sure each note would be the last. The dreaded gong never rang. Although six other contestants had sung her selection—"O Mio Fernando," from Donizetti's opera *La Favorita*—she was the first one allowed to complete it, trill and all. Thunderous applause burst from the audience, which consisted mostly of other contestants and their teachers.

"*Quiet, please, quiet,*" called a voice through the loudspeaker. "We told you at the beginning, no applause."

The clapping continued. When it finally stopped, Marian bowed and started to leave.

"Does the contestant have another song, please?" called a judge from the balcony.

"Yes," she answered. Handing the pianist the music, she sang an encore.

The first round was over. Marian was one of the sixteen out of three hundred contestants chosen to compete in the semifinals.

Back in Philadelphia, she continued her strict routine of work and practice, practice and work, through the hot month of June into a hotter July. It was so hot that she joined a swimming class at the Y.

The weeks passed quickly. Now she was in Aeolian Hall again, awaiting her turn in the semifinals.

"You won't have to wait so long today," said Mr. Boghetti. "Only sixteen contestants, and you're number ten."

Good, Marian thought, for her right ear throbbed with pain.

"Marian!" Boghetti shook her arm. "They're calling your name. Didn't you hear?"

"Yes, yes, of course." Marian walked to the stage and managed to sing in spite of the pain. When it was over, she could hide it no longer.

"My ear aches terribly, Mr. Boghetti," she said. "I'm going right home."

"Why didn't you tell me? Can you hear all right?"

"I—I think so. I'll call you later."

She wondered if she were going deaf. The thought made her tremble. If she couldn't hear, how could she sing?

Mother was waiting at the door when she arrived home. "Mr. Boghetti just called from New York," she said. "You've won the contest, dear. The judges thought you were so good, they canceled the finals!"

"That's nice."

"Nice? Is that all you can—"

"Excuse me, Mama. I'll be back in a few minutes." Before Mrs. Anderson could ask any questions, Marian ran to see Dr. Taylor.

"Your ear is badly infected," he announced, looking at it with a light. "Have you been putting something in it, young lady?"

"No, not that I can think of. Wait, I remember. I've been taking swimming lessons at the Y. I—I plugged up my ears with cotton to keep out the water. Is it serious, Doctor? Will I be deaf?"

Dr. Taylor smiled. "No," he said slowly. "You want to hear

47

yourself when you sing for the King of England, don't you? I'll cure your earache on one condition."

"What?"

"That you never take another swimming lesson as long as you live!"

Marian smiled and gave her promise. It wasn't hard to keep.

On the evening of August 26, 1925, Marian stood backstage at Lewisohn Stadium, awaiting the time for her solo. She wore a new light-blue evening gown she had bought especially for the occasion.

It was a balmy evening and the huge arena was filled, from the tables on the ground to the less expensive seats in the "rocks" at the top of the bowl. There were many white people in the audience, far more than usual. She was glad. She wanted to bring the glory of music to people of all races, not only her own. Many of her people were in the audience too: Mama, her sisters, relatives, friends, and well-wishers who shared her honor and prayed for her success.

"It's time for your first selection, Miss Anderson."

The musicians moved back to make a passageway, and she stepped to her place on the podium beside the conductor. She couldn't help feeling nervous. She had never sung with an entire symphony orchestra before, and that dreadful night at Town Hall kept returning to her mind. The audience started to applaud, even before she sang. Marian knew they were with her, and her throat relaxed.

The conductor tapped on his music stand. A hush fell over the big stadium, and Marian Anderson's rich, velvety voice soared over the audience to the darkening heavens above. When she had finished, she received a storm of applause. Even the musicians joined in by tapping bows on music stands.

Then it was time for an encore, and later in her second appearance on the program, she sang a group of spirituals. Billy was at the piano. The music of her people—"Deep

48

River," "Heav'n," and "Song of the Heart"—sounded more solemn and meaningful in nature's setting under the stars. The audience called for an encore, another, and the concert ran far into the night. When it finally ended, the bouquet of red roses in her arms seemed pale in comparison to the evening's splendor.

The reviews the next morning? Enthusiastic, but reserved, with *The New York Times* devoting but two or three inches to the entire affair.

> Miss Anderson made an excellent impression. She is endowed by nature with a voice of unusual compass, color, and dramatic capacity. The lower tones have a warm contralto quality, but the voice has the range and resources of a mezzo-soprano. In passages of sustained melody the singer showed a feeling for melodic lines, while in the aria, "O Mio Fernando," she gave evidence of instructive dramatic impulse. Miss Anderson also sang Negro spirituals.

The *New York Herald Tribune* had the following:

> A remarkable voice was heard last night at Lewisohn Stadium. Its possessor was Marian Anderson, a young Negro contralto, who was the only singer chosen from about three hundred contestants in the auditions held last June. She appeared as soloist last night before what was estimated as the third largest Stadium audience of the summer. About 7,500, with a good-sized Negro contingent, were included in this band of enthusiasts.

The reviewer went on to describe the beauty of her voice and how its natural power filled the enormous stadium with no difficulty at all. But behind the reviews was always the same thought: She has a beautiful voice, but the poor girl is colored. What can she possibly do about it?

What, indeed. There was *some* change in the nature of her engagements in the next few months, to be sure. Concert managers considered her singing on a par with well-established singers', and she received requests from Canada and the West Coast. Most significant was the fact that more and more

49

white people were coming to her concerts, even when she appeared in Negro schools in the South. Yet there was a long way to go.

Then something happened that might have been a turning point. She was appearing at Carnegie Hall one night as soloist with the Hall Johnson Choir, a group of renowned Negro singers. The audience was enthusiastic, and when the performance was over, a tall, heavyset man came to her dressing room. He was Arthur Judson, head of one of the top concert bureaus in the country. Marian knew he was on the Stadium Concert Committee. Had he been at Lewisohn the night she sang there?

Evidently not. His first words were: "Why, Miss Anderson, I didn't know you could sing like that!"

"Thank you."

He hesitated a moment, taking a cigar from his breast pocket. "I'm in a position to do a great deal for you, Miss Anderson. I think I can start you off at seven hundred and fifty dollars a concert." He put the cigar to his lips and struck a match. "If you're interested, that is."

Interested? Marian was taken aback. She had never earned anywhere near that much. As excited as she was, her face remained calm. "Yes," she said evenly, "I am interested."

"Good. Can you come to my Philadelphia office?"

"Would Tuesday morning be all right?"

Seven hundred and fifty dollars a concert! If money were the measure of success, perhaps she was on her way.

Boghetti insisted on going to Judson's office with her. "Now remember," the voice teacher whispered, as the receptionist showed them in, "sign nothing until we have time to talk about it."

Mr. Judson sat behind a big mahogany desk, talking on the phone. Marian glanced at the pictures of famous singers on the walls.

"To Arthur, to whom I owe my success," was written on one of the photographs.

"Thank you, Arthur," was written on another.

"Good morning, Mr. Judson. This is Giuseppe Boghetti, my voice teacher," Marian said when Mr. Judson finished talking.

"Oh, yes. How do you do?" They shook hands and settled back in their chairs and talked about the weather. Finally Mr. Judson got down to business. But now he was speaking in terms of five hundred dollars a concert instead of the seven hundred and fifty he'd mentioned Sunday. Obviously, he had thought it over or discussed it with his associates and decided he couldn't get the higher figure. Another disappointment: she would not, he said, be under his personal management. One of the other men in the office would handle her bookings.

Mr. Boghetti stood up, and the look in his eyes told Marian to do the same.

"Thank you, Mr. Judson," she said, folding the neatly typed contract he handed her. "I'll look this over and phone you in a few days."

She was disappointed, not about the money as much as the fact that Mr. Judson didn't feel it worthwhile to manage her himself. Nevertheless, being known as a "Judson Artist" meant prestige, so with Boghetti's consent, she signed the contract.

The Judson office did lend her name prestige, but as it turned out, it made very little difference in her career. When the year was over, she found she'd actually made fewer appearances than before. Although her fees had gone up, so had her expenses. She paid Billy more, and was happy to, but she was also expected to pay for expensive circulars and leaflets the Judson office prepared. So, though there were a few outstanding engagements, neither her income nor her status in the musical world had changed much. She and Billy were on the same old treadmill—churches, schools, small concert halls. She didn't blame the Judson office. They had discovered, no doubt, that a Negro singer in this country wasn't exactly in demand in the higher echelons of music. Roland Hayes was the exception, but he had reached the top only after estab-

51

lishing a fine reputation in Europe. For Americans looked to the Old World for guidance in the arts, and Europeans usually judged a performer on talent alone, not the color of his skin. Naturally enough, Marian thought about going to Europe. She asked Mr. Judson what he thought of the idea.

"No," he said, "I don't think you should."

"What *do* you suggest?"

"Well, as a matter of fact, Miss Anderson, I was talking to a friend of mine about you the other day. She knows a great deal about singing, and she seems to think you're not a contralto at all, but a soprano."

Marian's eyes widened. "I've always been a contralto," she said calmly. "All my teachers have said so."

"Nevertheless, I'd like you to sing for my friend. If she still says you're a soprano, that's how you'll be billed from now on."

Marian was upset. Although her voice covered three octaves, she knew she was a contralto. To call herself a soprano would be a mistake. How could Mr. Judson question her about such a basic thing? Didn't he have any confidence in her? "Thank your friend for her interest," she said quietly, "but I shall continue as a contralto." Smiling, she stood up and left the office.

A few months later Mr. Judson made a suggestion she did take, to study for a while with Frank La Forge, a singing coach who had a fine reputation for guiding successful young singers. Before she started with La Forge, she told Mr. Boghetti. "Of course I want to continue with you too," she added.

Boghetti's face turned red. "I don't see why you need two vocal teachers at once," he said, and she knew his pride was hurt.

"You're probably absolutely right," she said gently, "but perhaps this time I should do as Mr. Judson suggests, if only to please him."

"Then do not come back to me until you have finished with

La Forge." Boghetti's mind was made up. Nothing she said could change it.

Marian was sorry. She would miss her friend Boghetti, but Mr. Judson had suggested she study with La Forge only for a year or so. She didn't feel she could pass up any opportunity that might mean progress.

She was sitting in La Forge's studio waiting her turn one afternoon when a woman's voice came floating down the stairs. The woman was singing in German, and she seemed to understand the language so well that words and music blended perfectly.

Marian Anderson sang her German by rote—the reviewer had said about her recital at Town Hall, and again she thought of going to Europe. A few weeks later something else happened that made her want to go more than ever. She was singing a German song in a recital at La Forge's studio.

"Zum reinen wasser er mich weist . . . ," she sang. She caught her breath. She couldn't remember the next line. What to do? Stop? Start over? Instead, she substituted other words for those she had forgotten. Perhaps no one in the audience noticed the substitution. At least no one mentioned it. But at that moment, Marian made up her mind to learn German fluently, no matter how far she had to travel to do it.

Mr. La Forge didn't discourage the idea of going to Europe. Neither did Billy. When her time with La Forge was up, and she was seeing Boghetti again, he also encouraged the trip. "If you remain here," he said, "it will be merely a question of time before your early momentum is forgotten, and you'll be lost in obscurity. Europe is your only chance."

The people at church wanted her to go, and her sisters gave her courage by assuring her they would look after Mother. Mama herself was understanding. She knew what Marian meant when she said she was "going stale," repeating the same engagements year after year. She would miss her daughter, but above all, she wanted her to be happy.

Mr. Judson remained opposed to the whole idea. "If you

53

go to Europe," he said, "it will be to satisfy your vanity."

"Then," Marian replied, "I shall go for that purpose."

But to which country? Germany, to study German? France? Italy? England? She couldn't possibly afford them all. She asked Lawrence Brown, the pianist who had gone abroad with Roland Hayes.

"England would be best," he said. "Raimund von Zur Mühlen lives there now. He's a fine teacher of lieder,[1] and I'll be glad to write him and recommend you as a pupil."

Marian was delighted. Nothing could be better. She'd be in an English-speaking country, yet she could study German. Billy thought England best, and he wrote about her to Roger Quilter, a young English nobleman, who composed music and befriended promising young musicians, regardless of race.

"You're to call Mr. Quilter the minute you get to London," Billy instructed. "He'll know of a private home where you can stay. Lawrence Brown and Roland Hayes walked their feet off—"

"I see." Marian made up her mind to call Mr. Quilter as soon as she arrived in London.

Weeks later, Marian stood on deck of the *Ile de France*, waving good-by to her family. She'd taken enough money from the bank to pay for second-class passage and expenses, leaving the rest to take care of things at home. The big ship moved slowly away from the pier, and the tiny figure of her mother grew smaller and smaller. Horns tooted . . . whistles blew. . . . Mama joined in the excitement by gaily waving a handkerchief, but Marian was sure her lips were moving in prayer.

---

[1] German poems set to music.

6

THE weather was fine while Marian was on board ship with calm seas, clear skies, and afternoons warm enough to sit on deck in the sunshine. Most of the other passengers were white Americans, and though they weren't unpleasant, they didn't go out of their way to be friendly. Despite the moments of loneliness, the trip was a pleasant experience, and many amusing things happened along the way. She was sitting at her table in the elegant dining salon one evening, when her French waiter set a thick, juicy-looking steak before her.

"*Bon appétit!*" he said.

He needn't have. The sea air took care of her appetite. Thanking him, she cut into the steak eagerly. She hesitated, her fork in midair, for the meat was red inside, almost raw.

"Something is wrong, Mademoiselle?" said the hovering waiter. "Your steak—it is not to your taste?"

"I must admit I do like it well done—"

"*Well done? Ooo la la!*" He swept up her plate and stalked off to the kitchen, returning a few minutes later with the steak brown and crispy, the way she liked it.

"Thank you. That's much better."

"H'mmm." The waiter popped the cork off a bottle of wine.

"No, thank you. I don't care for any."

"*Mon dieu!* Burnt meat—no wine—Mademoiselle, you could never be the wife of a Frenchman!"

Marian laughed. Nothing could be farther from her mind.

A couple of evenings later, she stood on deck by the railing, enjoying the beauty of the moonlight reflected on the water below.

"Bon soir, Mademoiselle, c'est une belle nuit, n'est-ce-pas?"

She turned. Here was a chance to practice her high school French. Standing at her elbow was the Frenchiest-looking Frenchman imaginable—from spats on his feet to beret on his head!

"Oui," she said. Summoning her courage: *"Regardez ce soleil."*

"Soleil?" The gentleman looked puzzled. His lips turned up. His mustache quivered. He started to laugh.

Why was he laughing? It dawned on her at last. They were standing in the moonlight, and she had told him to look at the sun! Cheeks burning, she excused herself and hurried to her cabin to recover from her embarrassment.

Next day the ship docked at Southampton and before disembarking, she organized her luggage. It would be checked through customs, so she didn't have to worry about that. She shuffled through her pocketbook. Everything was there, passport, traveler's checks, address book, letter of credit for when her traveler's checks ran out. Her pocketbook was full, though, so she transferred some of its contents to her music case.

On shore everything went smoothly. She breezed through customs like a seasoned world traveler, changed a few American dollars into English money, and settled herself on the train for London. It was reassuring to know that Roger Quilter was expecting her. It would be almost midnight when she arrived. Closing her eyes, she dozed off, and next thing she knew, the train pulled into London's Paddington Station.

" 'elp you with your luggage, Miss?" asked a porter as she stepped out onto the platform.

"Yes, please." She handed him her baggage checks, and he returned with her valises a few minutes later.

" 'elp you find a cab, Miss?"

"Yes, but first I must make a call."

"Over 'ere, Miss." He led the way to a phone booth.

Stepping inside, she thumbed through her address book, and asked the operator to ring Roger Quilter's number.

The phone rang. And rang. And rang. At last a man answered.

"Hello," she said, "this is Marian Anderson. I have just arrived from America."

"Who?"

"Marian Anderson."

"Sorry, I do not know you."

"Is this Mr. Quilter?"

"No, Madame."

"Who is it, please?"

"The butler, Madame."

"May I speak to Mr. Quilter, please?"

"No, Madame, Mr. Quilter is not at home."

"Did he leave a message for me?"

"No, Madame. Mr. Quilter is in a nursing home."

Nursing home! He must have fallen ill suddenly and forgotten she was coming. "I see," she said weakly. "Well, thank you." What to do now? Try to find a hotel room? She didn't know where to begin. "Lawrence Brown and Roland Hayes walked their feet off," Billy had said. Still in the booth, she flipped through her address book. *Payne, John, 17 Regents Park Road, London.* John Payne was the Negro actor who'd once visited the Anderson home in Philadelphia; he lived in London now. Perhaps he could help.

" 'ave you finished, Ma'am?" asked the porter.

"Not quite—one more call." She lifted the receiver and called Mr. Payne's number. But actors travel as much as singers. Maybe he wouldn't be home either.

"Hello—" She recognized his deep voice at once.

"This is Marian Anderson from Philadelphia, Mr. Payne. Do you remember me?"

"Of course. Where are you?"

"Here in London at Paddington Station. I'm terribly sorry

to have to call you so late." She told him what had happened.

Mr. Payne's voice assumed the tone of a captain issuing a command. "Get into a taxicab. Come right over," he ordered. Gently he added: "My wife and I have a spare room—it's yours for as long as you like."

"Thank you so much. I'll be there as soon as I can."

She hung up and followed the impatient porter to a taxicab. Speeding through the quiet streets of London, she peered out of the window, trying to catch a glimpse of the famous landmarks she had heard about—Westminster Abbey, London Bridge, Piccadilly Circus. Between darkness and fog, she couldn't see a thing. She turned her head to look out of the back window. Odd there wasn't any. Sightseeing would have to wait. She sat back and relaxed until the taxi pulled up in front of the Paynes'.

"Come in! We're glad to see you." Mr. and Mrs. Payne helped her with her luggage, and in no time she was settled before a cozy fire, chatting and sipping a cup of tea.

"You must be done in, my dear," Mrs. Payne said, after a bit. "We'll have lots to talk about tomorrow. Come along. I'll show you to your room."

Marian smiled gratefully. She *was* tired. Picking up her pocketbook, she reached for her music case. It was gone. "A flat black case," she said, "did you see it?"

Mr. and Mrs. Payne tossed aside pillows, poked under chairs. "Are you sure you had it when you came in?"

"I—I don't know. Maybe I didn't—"

"There's a music shop up the street—"

"There were other things in it too," Marian explained, trying to keep calm. "Traveler's checks and my letter of credit— all I have in my pocketbook is the few pounds I exchanged at Southampton."

"My word. Do you suppose you left the case in the taxi?"

"Perhaps. Now all I have to do is find the taxi—wait, that shouldn't be hard. I remember—it was most unusual—there was no window in back!"

Mr. Payne smiled indulgently. "I hate to tell you this, Marian, but few taxis in London do have back windows. Look, it's late. Get a good night's sleep. We'll try to locate your case in the morning."

"Yes, of course." Marian followed Mrs. Payne upstairs, but sleep was out of the question. Tossing and turning, she tried to remember every move she had made. She was sure she had the case on the train. At least she thought so. How could she have been so careless?

When the first rays of light filtered through the window, she started to get up, but she lay back and forced herself to stay in bed. She was inconveniencing the Paynes enough already; she wouldn't upset their sleep too. When she heard someone stirring at last, she rose, dressed quickly, and joined Mrs. Payne in the kitchen.

"Good morning, Marian. Sleep well?"

She had to admit she had not.

"Let's sit down and have a nice English breakfast. I suggest that you do nothing else today but try to locate your case."

"I don't think I could do anything else."

Mr. Payne appeared in the doorway. "Today," he announced solemnly, "we shall go to Scotland Yard."

Marian was unable to keep from smiling. He sounded so British. She soon found out he had become British in other ways. He'd adjusted to the British tempo of life—doing things "in all good time." Breakfast was long and leisurely. There was a fire to build, his pipe to fill, morning papers to read. By then it was lunchtime. Lunch over, he took umbrella in hand and indicated he was ready to go. No, not quite. First he had to stop and introduce Marian to the neighbors, relating the saga of the lost music case to each and every one.

At last, at three o'clock, Mr. Payne and Marian entered Scotland Yard. It wasn't a yard, she discovered, but rather an ordinary office building and not nearly so exciting as in detective stories. To make her disillusionment complete, the lost-and-found officer reported that no music case had been brought in to that department.

"Perhaps it would be best to go back to the station and find my porter," she said. "Maybe he can lead me to the taxi."

"What did your porter look like?" asked Mr. Payne.

"I don't remember, but I'll recognize him by the way he speaks. He doesn't pronounce his 'H's'!"

Mr. Payne smiled. "My child, you've got a lot to learn about England. I know of no Cockney who does pronounce his 'H's'. Come along. We'll have a go at it."

They went to the station and walked up and down the platform, peering into the face of every porter who passed. It was no use, and they were about to give up, when a bobby approached.

"Looking for someone?" he asked.

Marian told him her problem. "Have you tried the Lost Property Office?" He pointed his shillelagh at a door on the other side of the platform.

"I didn't think of that!" With Mr. Payne at her heels, Marian hurried inside.

"Black music case?" The man in charge reached into a partition in the wall. "Would this be it?"

"Yes! Where—?"

"In a telephone booth. Someone turned it in."

"Of course! That's exactly where I left it."

A few days later Marian went to see Raimund von Zur Mühlen, the man Lawrence Brown had recommended to teach her German lieder. Von Zur Mühlen, or Master, as he was called, lived in Steyning, a tiny village about fifty miles from London. The train ride through the rolling hills and quiet valleys of Sussex reminded her of the farming country in her native Pennsylvania. England was lovely, and with no segregation laws she could easily understand why so many Negro artists from America decided to stay here. But not Marian. America was her home and always would be.

After renting a room in Steyning, she went to see Master at once. Bent with age, he sat in a big chair, a woolly red blanket over his knees, a gnarled cane at his side.

"So you are Marian Anderson," he said, his voice thick with a strong German accent. "Lawrence Brown wrote me you want to sing the German lieder."

"Very much," Marian replied.

Master pounded the floor with his cane. A young man appeared and sat down at the piano.

"Give him your music," said Master. "Let us begin."

Marian handed the pianist the music for "Im Abendrot," one of her favorite songs. He played the introduction. She began to sing. When she finished, there followed an awkward moment of silence. "Come here, please."

She crossed the room and sat down at Master's side.

"Do you know what the song you sang means?" he demanded, putting on his monocle, as if to see her better.

"Not every word. But I know what it's about."

"It is not enough to 'know what a song is about.' Sing something else, something you know all about."

This time she sang "My Lord, What a Morning," one of the spirituals she'd learned at church. Before she was halfway through: "Stop! You are singing like a queen, and I have not yet crowned you!"

Marian started studying with Master at once, but unfortunately after two lessons, he became too ill to teach. Saddened and disappointed, she returned to the Payne home in London. There she was cheered a bit because waiting for her was mail from home. Everything was fine in Philadelphia, Mama wrote; Ethel was still keeping company with that nice Jimmy de Priest; Alyce was going out a lot and becoming interested in politics; they all missed her and hoped she was well.

The second letter was from King. For years Boghetti had been saying: "Neither man nor contralto was meant to live alone. Marry a man who will make you happy." She had known since she had met him that King was that man. But there was so much to do. Right now, for example, she had to find another teacher. Perhaps Roger Quilter could recommend one. She phoned to see if he were home yet. Mr. Quilter *had* recovered from his sudden illness and was most anxious to help her in any way he could. He *did* know a teacher of German lieder—Mark Raphael, a former pupil of Master's. He would speak to him at once. And within the week Marian started her lessons with Raphael. She enjoyed them and felt she was making progress, but she was disappointed she could not study with Master himself.

Roger Quilter helped her in many ways. His spacious home was a meeting place for composers, musicians, and society people from all over England, and in the next few months he often invited Marian to sing for his guests. They liked her voice so much, they persuaded her to give a recital at Wigmore Hall. The recital was successful and the reviews complimentary, but nothing exciting happened as a result.

By now Marian had been abroad a year. Her money was running low, her spirits even lower. She longed for Mama's quiet understanding, her sisters' gay companionship, and she admitted to herself that she would like to see King. She decided to go home.

CHAPTER

7

AS THE big ocean liner steamed into New York harbor, Marian stood by the railing and gazed across the water at the Statue of Liberty. It was good to be home.

"Miss Anderson, would you follow me, please?" said the purser. "There's a gentleman coming to meet you on that tender." He pointed toward a small boat pulling up alongside the ship.

"Do you know the gentleman's name?"

"Sorry, the radio operator didn't say."

"Oh." Marian hoped it would be King. Her heart quickened at the thought.

It wasn't King, but another young man she had dated a few times before leaving the country. "What a nice welcome!" she said, as he placed a bouquet of roses in her arms. But she wished King had met her instead.

A few days later she did see King. He came to Philadelphia to visit her. He acted rather cool, and she tried to figure out why. Had he heard about the other fellow meeting her boat? Dear King, she said silently, don't you know you mean more to me than anyone else ever could? But as always, her career was uppermost in her mind. She had a long way to go before she could think of getting married, so she talked gaily about her travels and avoided any subject that might lead to seriousness. And as King, proud and handsome, walked out of the door, she wondered if she would ever see him again.

She had other visitors during that first week at home. Friends, neighbors, and people from church gathered in the parlor of the Anderson home every evening, eager to hear where she'd been, what she'd seen. With Mama gently urging her on, she told them about her voyage, sight-seeing in England, the people she had met. As for her career, there was little to tell. Anyway, she was much more anxious to hear what had been happening at home.

One morning, when she was settled and rested, she went to the Judson office to look at her schedule for the forthcoming season. The engagements they had arranged remained run-of-mill, in churches, theaters, small concert halls. Hadn't her European trip made any difference? No, she was told. If she'd sung for the King of England or been a great success in a famous, glamorous concert hall, it might have been different.

It was discouraging. She did not have much to show for her year abroad. She had learned a smattering of German, had a few brief reviews in London papers, and she wasn't as shy as she used to be. There was no use worrying about what might have been. What to do next was the important thing.

A manager named Sol Hurok was tops in the musical world now. He had a fine reputation for being courageous, progressive, and presenting the finest talent to the American public with taste and ingenuity. He'd handled great artists like Anna Pavlova, the Russian ballerina; Efrem Zimbalist, the violinist; Feodor Chaliapin, the opera singer. Perhaps Mr. Hurok's management was what she needed, and so she phoned his office to make an appointment.

Mr. Hurok was out of town or busy or in conference, his secretary said each time Marian called. An appointment was impossible. Obviously, Mr. Hurok wasn't interested.

Marian knew there was one thing left to do, and that was to go back to Europe as soon as possible. This time she'd go right to the source of German music, Germany itself. The question of how long it would take to save enough money was answered a few weeks later. She was singing in Chicago one night for

Alpha Kappa Alpha, a Negro sorority, when one of the girls said a gentleman wished to see her. His name, Marian thought the girl said, was Mr. Raphael.

Raphael! Mark Raphael, the man who had coached her in England when Master got sick. When the concert was over and the gentleman arrived, she discovered he wasn't Mark Raphael, but a Mr. *Ray Field*, who represented the Julius Rosenwald Fund, established by a wealthy Chicago businessman to help improve educational opportunities for Negroes.

"I enjoyed your performance very much, Miss Anderson," said Mr. Field. "What are your plans for the future?"

"I've been thinking of going to Germany to study—"

"I think you should," said Mr. Field. "You'll have to fill out the proper forms, of course, but I believe I can safely promise that the Fund will pay for your studies there!"

A way will be found, Mama had always said. This time she was right.

Getting used to Germany was much harder than getting used to England. Marian did not know a soul, and from the moment she stepped off the train, she was surrounded by strangers speaking a language she barely understood. To make matters worse, the Judson office had asked a German concert manager named Mr. Walter to meet her at the station, and Mr. Walter didn't appear. She found a hotel room herself, and phoned and asked Mr. Walter to meet her in the lobby. When two men arrived at the stipulated time, she assumed they were Mr. Walter and his partner.

"Good afternoon," she said in her carefully memorized German.

"Who are you?" the taller man asked.

"Marian Anderson," she replied.

The men shrugged their shoulders. The name obviously meant nothing to them.

"Judson," she said, thinking that would surely ring a bell.

"Judson?" said the taller man.

65

"Judson?" said the shorter. They had never heard that name either.

The hotel clerk came to her rescue. He spoke to the men in German and turned to Marian. "These men are in the cuckoo clock business," he reported. "You must have called the wrong Walter."

"Cuckoo? Oh dear—" Marian apologized as best she could. But when the two men left, she was sure they considered her in the same category as their clocks!

The right Mr. Walter was found at last, and when Marian explained that she couldn't afford to live in a hotel, he arranged for her to rent a room in a private home. She'd *have* to learn German, for her landlady, Frau von Edburg, understood no English. With the help of a pocket dictionary and much gesturing of hands, they managed to communicate.

Later Marian bought a simple language book and asked Herr von Edburg, a German actor, to help her. Together they pored over the book, Herr von Edburg placing his big hand over the English translations, so that she could read only the German. It was a hard way to learn, but when she turned to German music again, she discovered she knew quite a bit. She realized that as many times as she had sung German songs —Schubert's "Ave Maria," for example—she hadn't known the deepest meaning of the words. Now she felt she did.

But learning the language wasn't her only reason for coming to Berlin. She needed musical guidance as well, so she embarked on a course of study with Michael Raucheisen, a teacher who had been highly recommended. She was having a lesson with Raucheisen one spring afternoon in 1931 when two strange men came into the studio, sat down quietly, and waited for her to finish her song.

"I am Rulle Rasmussen, a concert manager from Norway," said the first man. "This is Kosti Vehanen, a pianist from Finland."

Mr. Vehanen, a shorter, plumper man with thinning hair, smiled. "We're looking for new talent," he explained in German, "and we've heard a great deal about Miss Anderson."

"Would you be available to sing some concerts in Scandinavia, Miss Anderson?" asked Mr. Rasmussen.

"Perhaps," she replied.

"If you do come to Scandinavia, this gentleman will accompany you on the piano." Mr. Rasmussen nodded toward Mr. Vehanen. "But before we make any definite arrangements, we'd like to hear you sing some more."

"I'm singing a recital at the Kaiser's old palace tonight. Would you care to come?"

"We certainly would."

Marian's grant from the Rosenwald Fund was running low, and as she walked down the lovely Unter den Linden and over the canal to the old palace, used now as a museum and school, she thought how marvelous it would be if the gentlemen liked her singing well enough to arrange some engagements in Scandinavia.

Entering the rear door of the palace, she passed a spacious hall, and continued down a dark corridor to the small classroom reserved for her recital. The two gentlemen had already arrived and were sitting on a low bench in back. Although they didn't look too comfortable, they remained in their seats after everyone else had left.

"I am certain I want you to come to Norway," said Mr. Rasmussen, unfolding his long legs and standing up. "You'll hear from me soon about final arrangements."

Kosti Vehanen stood by silently. He spoke little English, and he hadn't understood a word of the Negro spirituals Marian had sung. He'd never heard such music before, music from sighing fields of cotton, expressing the agony of the slave in the South. But although he didn't understand the words, Marian's voice delighted him. "I cannot forget the colors in her voice," he said. "Not only one color, but hundreds. If she succeeds in using all those colors to deepen the meaning of each word, she will be marvelous."

For the next few weeks Marian eagerly awaited word from Norway. It was more important than ever to get the Scandinavian engagements. Hoping to get good reviews, she had used what was left of her Rosenwald grant to give a concert at Bachsaal, Berlin's famous concert hall, named for Johann Sebastian Bach.

What a test of her newly learned German! For the first time, she sang German lieder to an audience that probably knew most of the words by heart. Apparently they were pleased. They applauded loudly, and dozens of people came backstage to meet her.

Her feeling of success was short-lived. Next day, not one paper in Berlin even mentioned the concert.

"Why?" she asked the von Edburgs. "Was my German that bad?"

"*Nein*," said Herr von Edburg. "You did fine."

"Then—?"

"In Germany, it is different from America. The critics here are in no hurry," he explained. "Be patient, Fräulein. The reviews will appear in a week or so."

Marian laughed with relief, and before the week was out, the reviews did appear. Most of them were complimentary, and the others— As Mama always said, you can't please everyone!

The long-awaited letter from Norway arrived soon afterward. Everything was arranged, Mr. Rasmussen wrote. Marian would appear in concerts in Oslo, Norway; Stockholm, Sweden; and Helsinki, Finland, one concert in each city, and a second if the first were successful. On the way to Oslo, however, Mr. Rasmussen decided she should stop and sing in a city called Stavanger at the mouth of the Bokn Fjord. The audience there seemed pleased, so he arranged a similar concert in the rainy city of Bergen, birthplace of the famous Norwegian composer, Edvard Grieg.

From there they went on to beautiful Oslo, where audiences were so enthusiastic that a second concert was held at once.

In Sweden, Marian's appearances were handled by Director Enwall, Rasmussen's colleague. Mrs. Enwall and Marian became close friends, and together they went shopping for a gown for Marian's second concert in Stockholm.

"White will emphasize your beautiful color," Mrs. Enwall said, and she persuaded Marian to buy a white crepe gown with a small train. But the train, though fashionable, made Marian feel self-conscious. "It's just too much," she said, and she cut it off.

The Swedes didn't take Marian to their hearts as quickly as the Norwegians, but Director Enwall explained that Swedes are naturally more cautious. Once they had accepted her, their approval would be everlasting.

Now they continued on to Kosti Vehanen's home in Helsinki, Finland. Here Kosti, a well-trained musician, became Marian's accompanist, and his musicianship and knowledge of European languages helped her enormously.

Her first rehearsal with Kosti was memorable. He began by playing softly, as if to catch the pulse of her voice. Then she sang her first tone. He wondered where the tone came from. Later he said: "It was as though the room had begun to vibrate, as if the sound came from under the earth. I could not find the direction of the tone, but it seemed to me that the very atmosphere was charged with beauty. . . . Then the sound swelled to majestic power, the flower opened its petals to full brilliance; and I was enthralled by one of nature's rare wonders!"

After Helsinki, Marian and Kosti appeared in Copenhagen, Denmark, where Marian felt almost as much at home, as welcome and comfortable, as with her own people. Here in Scandinavia, she was accepted as an individual, judged for her qualities as a human being and an artist, not for the color of her skin. Scandinavians came to her hotel to visit her, invited her to their homes, sent flowers and notes. How different from the coolness she'd often met on her concert tours at home—the segregation laws, the hotels and restaurants that refused to serve her, or hotels that admitted her but requested that she not invite her Negro friends to visit!

She wasn't paid a great deal for this first Scandinavian tour, only seventy-five or a hundred dollars a concert, but the tour meant much more than money alone. It made her realize she could be a success although she was Negro.

Her six months in Europe were coming to an end, and the Judson office had her engagements lined up for the next season. So, saying good-by to her new Scandanivan friends, she sailed for home.

This time her European trip should surely make a difference. Again she was disappointed. News of her Scandinavian successes had reached home before she did, and yet American managers were unimpressed. Her schedule was similar to the others—schools, churches, small concert halls.

"Why?" she asked Mr. Judson.

"Because Americans look to Paris or London or Vienna for musical guidance. Not Oslo, Helsinki, or Copenhagen."

"I see." Marian was discouraged. Her trip had made no difference in her career at home, but it had been worthwhile. She'd made wonderful friends in Scandinavia, and whether Americans looked to them for musical guidance or not, she cherished their friendship. She was touring when she received a cablegram from Director Enwall.

"Can offer you twenty concerts," he said. "When can you come?" She would have to think it over. Meantime, a second cablegram arrived.

"Can offer you *forty* concerts."

Then still another: "Can offer you *sixty*."

Marian laughed. If she didn't know Director so well, she'd think he was playing games. She replied that she would return to Scandinavia when her current tour was over, but that she would accept his first offer of twenty concerts. After that, she'd come back to America to fulfill her commitments here. Mr. Enwall agreed, and when her current tour was over, she sailed

70

for Europe again. Before sailing, she made one additional appearance not listed on her itinerary. With her mother and sisters sitting proudly in the front row, Marian Anderson, home from her travels abroad, sang with the choir at the Union Baptist Church, at the corner of Fitzwater and Martin Streets, in South Philadelphia!

8

MARIAN was pleased to be back in Scandinavia. The atmosphere was as warm and friendly as the climate was cold and exhilarating. Under Kosti's guidance she added more Scandinavian music to her repertoire—songs written by Sibelius, Grieg, Kilpinen. It was beautiful music, but different, mysterious, and she was not sure she sang it well. She'd been practicing a Sibelius song, "Norden," for weeks, and one night in Helsinki she finally decided to sing it in public for the first time.

As Kosti played the introduction, she looked out at the audience. They recognized the tune; she could tell by the expressions on their faces. They were probably wondering how this stranger from a far-off place, a member of a different race, could sing their beloved Sibelius. So indeed was she. Eyes closed to blot everything but music from her mind, she sang, trying to pronounce each word as Kosti had taught her. When her last tone faded away, there was a moment of silence, and then thunderous applause. The Finns were delighted with her rendition of Sibelius, the composer they loved so much they celebrate his birthday as a national holiday. The Finns were delighted, but not Marian. She felt there was room for improvement.

"If only I could sing for Sibelius himself," she said to Kosti. "I am sure he could help me understand his music better, so I could sing it with more feeling."

72

"I shall try to arrange it," Kosti replied.

A few days later, they received word that they could spend one half hour with the seventy-year-old composer, enough time for Marian to sing a few songs and chat a bit.

It was dusk when they arrived at Sibelius' villa, deep in the forest north of Helsinki, and the house seemed aglow with candlelight.

Sibelius himself greeted them, his wife at his side. "Welcome to our home," he said. He turned to his wife and said, "Aino, dear, please, some coffee for our guests!"

"Yes, of course—" Mrs. Sibelius hurried away.

"I have heard so much about you, Miss Anderson. I must hear you sing at once." Sibelius nodded toward the piano by the window and settled his big frame into an easy chair to listen.

Marian sang some of his music. When she finished, he stood up, strode across the room, and threw his arms around her. "The ceiling of my home is far too low for you," he exclaimed. Marian wondered if he meant her height or her voice.

As his wife returned with the coffee tray, he said: "No—no coffee—let us have champagne!"

Sibelius meant her voice; he felt it cause for celebration! So it was all over Scandinavia, from tiny Northern towns in the Land of the Midnight Sun to large cities farther south. Ticket sales broke records; crowds packed the concert halls and waited outside to catch a last glimpse of her. Marian's fans were so enthusiastic that police often had to escort her to the car. "Marian Fever" the critics called it, and the epidemic spread quickly. Tickets for her appearances were hard to obtain, and one night the conductor of the Finnish National Opera had to sit on the piano bench beside Kosti!

The President of Finland caught "Marian Fever" too, in a most unusual way.

Marian and Kosti were to give a recital in a village in central Finland one winter night. That afternoon they rehearsed in a tiny, snow-covered church outside the town. They were in the organ loft going through a song, when Marian heard the shuffling of feet downstairs. A moment later a high-ranking officer appeared and whispered something in Kosti's ear.

"Who was that?" Marian asked when the officer left.

"Oh, no one," said Kosti. "Just an aide to the President of Finland."

"The *President?*"

"That's right. The President himself is downstairs with some of his staff. His aide wanted to know if they could stay and listen awhile. I told him it was all right."

"Gracious!" Marian reached up and touched the old brown hat she was wearing. "I can't let the President see me in this."

"I thought you said you were going to buy a new hat."

"I meant to. I guess I forgot."

"Never mind. Let's get back to work. I'm sure the President is far more interested in your voice than your hat."

When they finished rehearsing, the President was waiting for them at the foot of the stairs. "How do you do, Miss Anderson," he said warmly. "I wanted to thank you personally for letting us listen. We've been on an inspection tour of munitions plants, and we heard your voice from the window as we passed. We had to come in and see who it was. Imagine, finding such beauty in a silent church buried deep in winter's snow!"

"Thank you very much, Mr. President," said Marian. When he left, she said, "Oh dear, I simply must buy a new hat."

But when she returned to the city she was so busy that she didn't take time for shopping. Kosti made up his mind to get rid of the hat without hurting her feelings. His chance came at rehearsal one day, when she took it off, placed it on the piano, and closed her eyes to sing. Continuing to play with one hand, Kosti snatched up the hat and tossed it under the piano bench.

"Where's my hat?" Marian asked, when she was ready to leave.

"I don't see it," Kosti murmured, bending over his music

74

so she would not be able to see the expression on his face.

"Oh. Now I'll have to buy a new one."

Once she started to shop, she bought lots of other things until eventually she had a lovely wardrobe of smart, simple dresses for daytime and elegant gowns for evening. Marian became a lady of fashion, and women everywhere began to ask what she wore as well as what she sang.

She became more poised. Until now, she had always hidden her hands under a big kerchief when she sang. She thought they were large and clumsy.

"No," said Kosti. "Your hands are impressive, artistic," and he convinced her to leave them uncovered, clasped as if in prayer or raised to express the feeling of a song.

Marian became more worldly in other ways. It was going from Stockholm to Helsinki that she took her first airplane flight. As the plane rose into the sky, she peered out of the window at the archipelago below, set like sparkling jewels in the setting of the sea. Gradually, as they flew eastward, earth, sea, everything, vanished from sight. Marian caught her breath. Outlined clearly against the clouds was the tiny shadow of the plane; curving around the shadow was a beautiful, full-blown rainbow!

"Now I understand," she said softly. "If the good Lord doesn't like to behold the misery on earth, he covers it from his sight with clouds. But where there are human beings, there is always a dark shadow."

Kosti smiled. Marian might become a world-famous singer, a sophisticated continental traveler, but she would always remain the same religious girl who had sung in the choir at church.

Marian and Kosti flew from Stockholm to Helsinki on another occasion. This time they could see no islands, no sea, no rainbow, nothing but thick, woolly fog.

"We should have landed in Helsinki five minutes ago," Marian whispered, glancing at her watch.

"I know." Kosti looked toward the open door of the cockpit. The pilots were working feverishly, evidently trying to figure out their exact location. The motor slowed down; they began to descend.

"How can they see through the fog?" Marian asked as the plane dipped lower and lower.

"I—" Kosti gasped, and Marian followed his gaze to the window. They were about to hit a radio tower! Eyes closed, hands clasped, she prayed. The plane swerved and missed the tower by inches. Next came a scraping sound as wings brushed treetops, and up, up they went, then down again. The plane landed safely.

Eager to set foot on ground, Kosti and Marian hurried down the stairs. A gentleman came running across the field to greet them.

"—the Mayor of Helsinki," Kosti whispered.

"Miss Anderson! Mr. Vehanen!" said the Mayor. "I want to congratulate you on your safe arrival."

"Thank you, Mr. Mayor," said Marian.

"Perhaps we should all be thanking Marian for the safe landing," said Kosti. "I'm sure she prayed for it."

"I imagine everyone on the plane was praying," she said.

"They probably were," Kosti replied, smiling. "But somehow, I have the feeling that Marian Anderson's voice is heard before anyone else's!"

Marian was earning lots more money than she ever had before. She was able to send some back to her family, and for the first time in her life she could buy all the music she wanted and have it bound in leather.

"Mama," she wrote in a letter home, "at last I can give you something special, something you've dreamed about since you were a little girl. What would you like?"

Mrs. Anderson was thrilled with Marian's letter. But all she wanted, she wrote in reply, was that God should lift up people to understand and be kind and that he would hold Marian in the hollow of his hand.

76

Although Marian was earning more money than she ever had, she often sang for charity at big benefits in glamorous halls, in hospitals, orphanages, even in prisons.

One day she and Kosti were asked to give a concert at a penitentiary for life-term prisoners in Denmark.

"Are you frightened?" Kosti asked as they drove up to the sombre, dreary-looking prison buildings with their barred windows.

"No," said Marian. "Criminals are only people who have made mistakes."

"The people here have made some pretty big ones," said Kosti. And as Marian stepped in front of the audience in the prison chapel, she thought Kosti was probably right. Never in her life had she seen such sinister-looking faces. No wonder guards marched up and down the aisle with rifles pointed! Not only were the prisoners sinister-looking, Marian could tell by their expressions that they were skeptical. She had appeared before many skeptical audiences. She knew the look, raised eyebrows, set lips that seemed to say, "Please me, I dare you."

But generally, as she sang, eyebrows would lower, lips relax, as the people in the audience let themselves be carried away by the music. Not this time. The men's expressions remained unchanged. She knew she hadn't reached them. Marian sang a few more numbers, and as a final selection, a funny tune called "The Cuckoo."

That did it. Even the armed guards couldn't quell the applause. The men clapped on and on until one of the prisoners stood up and lifted his hand. "Now *we* shall sing for you," he announced.

And they did. Marian Anderson had brought music back to their hearts.

Traveling about Europe, Marian crossed the borders between many countries. Her most unusual border-crossing was from Finland into the Soviet Union.

"Look, Marian," said Kosti as the train clanged to a stop at the border. "That little river is the borderline. See? The Finnish half of the bridge is white. The Russian half, red."

Marian nodded and started to reply, but a gruff voice interrupted her. A Soviet officer stood in the middle of the aisle, his long finger pointing at the square black case on the seat beside her. "What is that?" he asked.

"My phonograph," she said. She opened it to show him.

"That?" He pointed to a package fastened on the inside of the lid.

"Some records."

"Why do you take records to the Soviet Union?" he demanded.

Marian hesitated, and Kosti came to her rescue. "This lady is Marian Anderson, the singer," he explained. "Those are recordings of her songs."

"H'mmm." The officer snapped the phonograph shut and picked it up by the handle. "Come with me," he ordered.

"Do you suppose they'll take my phonograph away?" Marian whispered as she and Kosti followed the officer off the train into the little wooden customs house.

Kosti shrugged.

Inside, the officer opened the phonograph, placed a record on the turntable, and wound it up.

"Sometimes I feel like a motherless child . . ." Marian's voice soared through the cold shack, filling every bleak corner with warmth and beauty. One by one the other officers gathered around to listen.

When it was over the officer asked, "How do we know it is your voice?"

Kosti looked grim. "I told you," he said. "This lady is a great concert artist. She's on her way to sing in Leningrad and Moscow. She—she—" Kosti began to sputter with anger.

Marian placed her hand on his arm. "It's all right," she said. Lifting her voice, she sang, "Sometimes I feel like a motherless child . . ." She paused.

"We are still not sure," said the officer. "Continue."

78

When that song was finished, he asked for another. "Thank you," he said. "Now we are sure." He closed the phonograph and gave it back.

"I think he knew who you were all the time," Kosti whispered, as he and Marian boarded the train. "He wanted a free recital!"

Apparently many other Soviets had heard about Marian. The halls were packed from her first concert in Leningrad to her last in Moscow.

"Don't sing religious songs or spirituals in Russia," Director Enwall had warned. "They'll fall on deaf ears."

"They are the songs of my people," Marian had answered. "I shall sing them whenever and wherever I please."

And she did.

Instead of announcing Schubert's "Ave Maria" ("Hail, Mary"), however, the announcer called it "An Aria by Schubert." That did not bother Marian. They could call it whatever they liked as long as she could sing it.

As Marian and Kosti were leaving the stage at the end of their first recital in the Soviet Union, suddenly there came an earsplitting noise. They turned to see the people from the back of the hall come rushing down the aisle; those in front pounded on the stage. "*Deep River! Heaven, Heaven!*" they called.

Marian bowed and sang an encore. More! they demanded, and Marian felt that the Russians' appreciation of music came from deep within their souls.

Usually concert halls in the Soviet Union were brightly lighted. But one night the whole hall was dark except for a powerful spotlight on Marian. During intermission, Kosti asked why, but no one seemed to know. Later someone whispered that Joseph Stalin, the Soviet dictator, was in the audience.

Between concerts Marian and Kosti did lots of sight-seeing. They saw Catherine the Great's Palace, Lenin's Tomb, and they attended an opera written by the famed Russian composer Shostakovitch. A few days later Shostakovitch returned the compliment by attending one of Marian's recitals, and during intermission he came to the artists' room to meet her.

Marian felt honored.

So did Shostakovitch.

At that time a thirty-ruble bill (about three dollars) was the highest denomination in the Soviet Union, and after a concert Marian and Kosti were often handed big bundles of money wrapped in newspaper or brown paper bags. The money had to be spent in Russia, so Marian had a shopping spree. She bought furs, jewelry, antiques, and some beautiful velvet capes that had once been used in Soviet churches. Sometime later a customs inspector on the border of Spain and France looked at the capes dubiously.

"What is this?" he asked, lifting one from her trunk.

"Miss Anderson's evening cape," Kosti answered.

The customs inspector ran his hand over the rich gold and silver embroidery. "You think I believe this girl wears capes as gorgeous as this?" he asked.

"This girl," said Kosti, "is a famous singer. She often wears this cape on her way to recitals."

"Doesn't she have any others besides those stolen from churches?"

"Stolen? What do you mean?"

"We had a wire from headquarters to watch out for such things. You shall both stay here." The cape over his arm, the inspector started to walk away.

"Wait—" Kosti rummaged through his suitcase and came up with a picture of Marian wearing the same cape in Stockholm.

"Oh, that's different." The inspector put the cape back in the trunk, closed the lid, and sent Marian and Kosti on their way.

Marian went to many parties in the Soviet Union. One special occasion was a supper given by Ippolitov-Ivanov, the

Russian composer. Ivanov, a jolly round man with a pointy beard, sat at the head of the table, holding a fork with a great long handle. Whenever one of the guests would finish his food, Ivanov would spear some meat with his fork, stretch it across the table, and fill the empty plate!

Before she left the country Konstantin Stanislavski, the world-famous Russian director and dramatic teacher, invited Marian to tea. Some of his actor-pupils were there, and they asked Marian to sing. When she finished, Stanislavski asked if she had ever thought of singing in opera, and Marian admitted she had.

"How would you like to stay in Moscow and be Carmen in my Moscow Art Theater Production?" he asked.

"That would be marvelous! But I have a tour to finish; then I must return to my own country."

When Marian and Kosti left Moscow a few days later, her seat on the train was filled with white lilacs, sent by Stanislavski. Lilacs in the middle of a cold Russian winter! Stanislavski must truly be a magician.

But a singer's life is not all parties and flowers and compliments. It's also storms and mud and waiting. When Marian and Kosti flew from the Soviet city of Tiflis to the famous oil city of Baku, a sudden storm forced their plane to land in an open field far from civilization. They waited for hours until they could take off again, and when they reached Baku at last, there was only one way to get to the waiting room, by wading through mud up to their knees. Sitting on a hard wooden bench, they waited again. And waited. And waited, until an open car appeared at last. As they jounced through the windy oil fields to the hotel, Marian's hat blew off—the one hat she had with her. The driver jammed on his brakes. Kosti jumped out and retrieved the flyaway hat, but not before it had fallen into a slimy pool of oil.

A weary, muddy, oil-soaked Marian arrived at the hotel. She bathed and dressed, and went onstage looking as if she had spent the day in quiet repose.

Several days later she experienced a rainy ride through the Caucasus Mountains in an open truck, crowded in with dozens of other passengers. On another day she flew in a private plane, with a pilot who insisted on doing stunts in the air. When they landed, she rode over rocky dirt roads by horse and rickety wagon to a sanitarium—the only place where rooms were available.

After the Soviet Union, she returned to Scandinavia. The more Marian sang, the more she was asked to sing, and before the year was out, her original twenty concerts had swelled to over a hundred. Sometimes she sang eight concerts in nine days; something a singer should not do. Yet Marian's voice was not strained. It sounded better than ever, and when the current concert season ended, Director Enwall urged her not to go home. "Stay in Europe a while longer," he said. "I'll arrange for you to sing in London, Paris . . ."

She couldn't resist. She wrote the Judson office asking if they would postpone her American engagements.

No, they wrote back. They could not. As an example of "engagements too important to postpone," they mentioned a date to sing for a sorority. Actually the Judson office had only ten engagements lined up for the whole season, every one the same caliber as before. Marian had been acclaimed by some of Europe's greatest connoisseurs of fine music, but in her own country, her status continued to remain the same.

"Cancel the engagements," she wrote Judson. After she had mailed the letter, misgivings set in. She'd cut one of the strongest chords binding her to her homeland, the professional one. For the first time she had no definite date on which she had to return to the United States. It was a lonesome feeling.

"Wouldn't you like to come to Europe?" she wrote her mother.

"Perhaps someday," Mama answered, "but how can I leave the children?"

"The children," Marian's sisters Ethel and Alyce, were grown women, and Ethel was married. Finally they convinced Mama they were old enough to be left on their own, and a few weeks later Marian met her mother at Le Havre. Never in her life had she been so glad to see anyone.

9

DIRECTOR Enwall arranged for Marian to sing in London, Paris, Vienna, Salzburg, and Geneva. Hitler had come into power, but most of the world was unaware of what was happening in Germany. When a request came to appear in the Berlin Philharmonic, Marian agreed to go.

"There is only one question," the Berlin concert master wrote in answer to Director Enwall's letter, "Is Miss Anderson one hundred percent Aryan?"

Arrangements with Berlin came to an end.

It was good to be in London again. Marian reminisced with the Paynes about the time she'd arrived in the middle of the night without her music case; she saw her old friend Roger Quilter and listened to his latest compositions. Although the British reviews had been brief and reserved, London felt like a second home.

After London, Marian left for gay, glamorous Paris. Foreign singers were no novelty there, and few Parisians came to Marian's first concert. Those who did, however, were wildly enthusiastic. *"Bravo! Bravissimo!"* they called, demanding one encore after another. And when her second concert was a sell-out, Mr. Horowitz, her Paris manager, suggested a third.

"But it's almost June," Marian said, "too late in the season for another concert. And don't you think two in one city are enough?"

"Not in Paris," said Mr. Horowitz.

Kosti nodded agreement and tried to persuade Marian all the way down the Champs-Élysées. They arrived at the hotel, and Marian was not yet convinced that a third concert was advisable. Kosti continued to discuss it through the lobby, into the elevator, and down the hall to her mother's room. When Mrs. Anderson opened the door and realized they were talking business, she slipped quietly outside.

"All right, Kosti," said Marian, "you can phone Mr. Horowitz and tell him to make arrangements for another concert." She opened the door and called her mother.

Kosti hung his head as if in shame. "Please excuse me, Mrs. Anderson," he said to Mama sheepishly. "I won't be bad any more."

"Shouldn't Marian do what she wants?" Mama asked, rising to her full height of five feet.

"Of course," Kosti replied, picking up the phone. "But Marian is a great artist. She owes it to the world to give as many people as possible the chance to hear her sing."

Time proved Kosti and Mr. Horowitz right in insisting on a third concert. Every Parisian who had come to the first or second concert came to the third, and brought along a friend! The program that night well demonstrated Marian's versatility. There was Schubert's "Bird Song," filled with long, high trills; an aria from a French opera; an ancient lullaby; a wild sailor's song Kosti had written especially for her; and as always, a group of Negro spirituals.

Marian was resting in the artists' room during intermission, when Mr. Horowitz appeared with a bald-headed man wearing horn-rimmed glasses.

"Marian," said Mr. Horowitz, "I would like you to meet—"

Marian was so excited she scarcely heard the man's name. She didn't have to, for she recognized him at once. It was Sol Hurok, the impresario she had tried to see in New York.

"How do you do, Miss Anderson," he said. "I'd like to speak

to you when you have more time. How about tomorrow morning? Would that be convenient?"

Marian agreed, and next morning she and Kosti met Mr. Hurok in Mr. Horowitz' office.

Mr. Horowitz sat to the left of his desk, Mr. Hurok behind it. What a big man he is, Marian thought. She realized that it wasn't his actual size that awed her, but the idea of what he could do for her. To be successful in her own country, she needed someone with enough courage to stand up to the prejudice that was holding her back. From what she'd heard, Mr. Hurok was that man. He took chances when he believed in an artist, even if odds were against him.

He wanted to know how many concerts she had been singing each season in the United States, and how much she had been paid for them. Marian answered his questions slowly, her voice breathless with excitement. She waited, hoping he'd give his opinion of last night's concert. He didn't, but he did say the words she'd been hoping to hear: "I might be able to do something for you." He thought he could guarantee fifteen concerts a season, and she could count on an advance, a specific sum of money before the American season started.

"That sounds fine, Mr. Hurok, but I'm not free to make definite arrangements with you. The Judson office has been handling my engagements."

"Have you a contract with them?" Hurok asked.

"Yes," said Marian. She remembered, however, that for some reason she had never signed it.

"Wire them," said Mr. Hurok. "Let me know as soon as you hear."

"Of course."

Marian and Kosti rose, said good-by, and left the office.

"Phew," said Kosti, "let's have a cool drink. We need the refreshment."

Marian agreed. Her heart was pounding as if she had run a race.

She didn't know it then, but their meeting had left Mr.

86

Hurok feeling much the same way. Years later he told of the first time he heard Marian sing. "Chills danced up my spine," he said, ". . . my palms were wet . . . I was shaken to my very shoes."

Marian cabled the Judson office at once.

No answer.

She wrote Mr. Judson a letter. Still no answer. She wrote another, and at last there came a reply, not from Mr. Judson, but from someone else in his office. They were sorry to lose her, they said, but she was free to sign with another manager if she wished. A few days later she signed a contract with Sol Hurok. It was decided she would return home in December, and Hurok would have some engagements lined up. "A colored contralto?" some of his associates said, when he got back to America and told them about her. "You won't be able to give her away."

In the meantime, news of her Paris success had spread, and many offers began to pour in from all over Europe. Managers flew to Paris from Italy, Spain, Belgium, to ask her to appear in their respective countries, and before long her schedule for the rest of the summer and fall was mapped out. She would appear in Belgium, Holland, Switzerland, Austria, Italy, Poland, and the Baltic countries.

"Marian," Mama said, "you have so many places to go, so much to do. I can't help you here, and I don't want to hinder you. If you don't mind, I'd like to go home."

"But you've only been in Europe two months," Marian protested. "Wouldn't you like to stay longer?"

"No. I have other children to look after. I'll be waiting for you when you come home." So Mama went back to Philadelphia and her other "children," and Marian continued her travels, piling one triumph on top of another.

Austria was especially memorable. So many composers whose music she loved had made Vienna their home sometime during their lives—Schubert, Beethoven, Mozart, Brahms, Haydn. She made a pilgrimage to every landmark she could find, from the white-gabled house where complaining neighbors forced Beethoven to change his apartment forty-five times to the cemetery where Beethoven, Brahms, Schubert, and Strauss were buried.

As she stepped onstage of the small hall in the Wiener Konzerthaus for her first Vienna appearance, she felt inspired. But the Viennese, proud of their glorious musical history, were slow to accept newcomers. The hall, although small, was almost empty. Then an amazing thing happened. When Marian returned to the stage after intermission, the empty seats were filled, and the hall was packed! Later she found out why. Another concert was going on in the larger hall next door, and during intermission the two audiences had mingled. Marian's audience had praised her so highly that many of the people from the larger hall came to hear the last half of her performance. A second concert was scheduled at once. Herbert F. Peyser, a critic on *The New York Times*, was in Europe at the time writing a series of articles on musical events. He wrote:

> . . . A sensation of the Vienna music season, and to date perhaps its most dramatic event, has been the debut here of the colored contralto from Philadelphia, Marian Anderson. In less than two weeks, she has given two recitals. The first was attended by a handful. The second was mobbed. It took only one number to effect such a conquest as has not been witnessed here in six months of Sundays. . . . It is by no means impossible to pick flaws in her work, to cavil at this trifle or that. To do so, however, is a great deal like criticizing the pyramids of Egypt because here and there a stone crumbled.

Another unheard-of thing happened in Vienna. Marian, who had sung over a hundred concerts without developing so much as a sniffle, came down with a cold. "The wonder has come to pass," Director Enwall wrote the concert master next on her itinerary. "Marian Anderson has a cold and must postpone her concert."

88

Soon Marian was up and off again. In July she appeared at the Salzburg Music Festival, held each year in the picturesque town high in the Austrian Alps.

Her first recital was held in the Mozarteum, named for Mozart, who was born in Salzburg. Again she appeared before a half-empty hall. One of her selections was "The Crucifixion":

> They crucified my Lord,
> And he never said a mumblin' word . . .
> not a word . . .
> not a word . . .

When it ended, the audience, music lovers who had come from afar, sat stunned in silence. Kosti, who had heard it many times, was too choked up to continue playing. "No one moved," he said. "I hardly dared close the music and open the next song, and when I finally did, my hand was trembling. It reminded me of the time Marian had sung in a Swedish church, where it was custom to wave handkerchiefs instead of applauding. Not a handkerchief was raised that day. Everyone in the audience was using his handkerchief to wipe away his tears!"

Word of Marian's artistry spread through Salzburg overnight, and an American woman named Mrs. Moulton, proud that a great artist like Marian came from the United States, arranged a recital for her in the ballroom of a local hotel. The guests included Arturo Toscanini and Bruno Walter, world-famous conductors; Lotte Lehmann, the renowned German singer; the Archbishop of Salzburg. Every leading light in the world of music who happened to be in Salzburg that summer came to see for himself if what he had heard about Marian was true. Vincent Sheean, the famous author, was there too.

"Hardly anybody in the audience understood English well enough to follow what she was saying," wrote Sheean, "and yet the immense sorrow—something more than the sorrow of a single person—that weighted her tones . . . her rapt and trancelike absorption in the music; her dark, angular beauty, all made the experience unlike any other. . . . A mantle of tragedy—that of an individual, of a race, of a destiny—seemed to envelop this artist and set her apart from all others. . . . After 'The Crucifixion,' . . . an electrical silence. I was myself paralyzed and could not have applauded if I had wished to do so. . . . Everybody else was in the same condition."

At the end of the performance Maestro Toscanini said he would like to meet her.

"Of course, Maestro," said the Salzburg manager. "I'll ask her to step down from the platform."

"Oh, no," retorted Toscanini, "I shall go up to see *her*."

Marian herself had no idea she'd just made musical history. When Maestro Toscanini appeared backstage, she was so surprised and excited that she scarcely heard a word he said. Later she was told that when he took her hand, the great maestro had murmured: "Miss Anderson, yours is a voice one hears once in a hundred years!"

After Salzburg, Marian continued her tour of Europe. She was welcomed, applauded, honored, wherever she went, from Geneva, where she was guest of honor at a dinner given by city authorities, to Rome, where she sang at the royal palace for four reigning queens. "Please," said the horrified major-domo, when she started to leave the room after her performance, "queens leave first!"

Once again it was almost time to return home. Her first concert, Mr. Hurok wrote, would be in New York on December 30, at Town Hall. Town Hall, the scene of her dismal failure thirteen years before. She had learned much since then. She had studied with the finest teachers in Europe, been applauded by heads of state, praised by Toscanini himself, and yet she could not forget her apprehension at the thought of Town Hall.

There was an important and painful decision to make. Who would be her accompanist in the United States? Master musician Kosti Vehanen, who had been such a help in developing her repertoire of fine music in many different languages? Or her old Philadelphia friend, Billy King?

Billy would understand if she decided on Kosti. But other Negroes might be offended. They would ask, why not give the opportunity to a member of our own race rather than a white man? She wouldn't blame them. Why should a young Negro musician work hard to become a good accompanist if no place was open to him? Furthermore, Mr. Hurok had written her that some people, particularly in the South, would object to a Negro woman appearing onstage with a white accompanist. She knew what Mr. Hurok said was true.

"But can't we try to change this prejudice?" Kosti asked. "I'm ready to do my part."

"It's too deeply rooted," Marian replied. "Two people can't solve it alone; it would take much time."

"Couldn't we at least try?"

Marian didn't answer. Kosti was from Finland, where there was no racial prejudice. It was impossible for him to understand how difficult and embarrassing the situation could be for both of them.

"Which comes first for you?" Kosti asked. "Music or the question of prejudice?"

Again Marian remained silent. No one was more anxious than she to promote better understanding between peoples. But how could she be most effective? Through the talent the good Lord had given her. Right now that talent was best nourished by Kosti's sound musicianship and knowledge of languages. She went to her desk, sat down, and wrote Mr. Hurok a wire:

"Mr. Vehanen and I arrive in New York on December 17."

10

THE decision was made to keep Kosti on as accompanist, and Marian tried to forget the matter. Mr. Hurok was worried about how the American public would accept a colored woman and a white accompanist. Only time would tell.

Marian was on her *sixth* trip across the Atlantic. Everyone working aboard the beautiful *Ile de France* knew Marian, from captain to cabin boy. On the first day out she and Kosti went to see the headwaiter about dinner reservations.

"Look," one fashionably dressed woman, who was also waiting, said to another, "there's Europe's famous singer, Marian Anderson. Poor girl—I wonder where she'll eat."

The headwaiter heard the remark. "A place of honor in the main dining room is reserved for Miss Anderson," he said, giving her his haughtiest headwaiter look. "You may dine in one of the smaller rooms, if you prefer."

"Oh, no—yes—that is, whatever you say."

"I'm sorry, Miss Anderson," said the headwaiter, when the women had left.

"That's all right," Marian replied calmly. "She didn't know better." On the third day out, Marian was relaxing on deck in a big steamer chair. She glanced at her watch. It was time to meet Kosti for rehearsal on the program for Town Hall. Throwing back her blanket, she got up and started down the nearest stairs. The sea was rough. Suddenly the ship lurched.

She clutched at the railing, but it was too late. Next thing she knew, she was lying at the bottom of the steel staircase, her left ankle throbbing with pain. Her first thought: would she be able to sing the concert? Her next thought: why not? Pulling herself up, she hobbled down the passageway to the rehearsal room, where she and Kosti had permission to use the piano.

"Marian!" Kosti cried. "What's wrong?"

"I stumbled—" she tried to smile. Pain made her wince instead. Kosti helped her to her stateroom and sent for the ship's doctor.

"Stay off your ankle, Miss Anderson," he ordered after his examination. "There's no X-ray on board, and I can't say for sure whether or not a bone's broken."

Marian remained in her stateroom for the rest of the day and the next. She had promised to sing at the ship's benefit that night, so wearing a long gown to cover her bandaged ankle, she was wheeled down a back passageway to the door of the music salon. She walked the short distance to the piano, sang, and went back to her stateroom. When they docked in New York, the doctor suggested she be wheeled down the gangplank. But not wanting to alarm her family and friends waiting on the pier, she wore her most comfortable shoes and limped down as best she could.

That night, the house in Philadelphia overflowed with relatives, neighbors, people from church who had come to hear about her travels and triumphs abroad. Marian was far more interested in catching up on the news at home than talking about herself. She was so happy to be there that she almost forgot her injured ankle. Next morning it ached worse than ever, and an X-ray showed the bone was fractured. With the Town Hall concert two weeks away, her leg had to be encased in a heavy plaster cast up to the knee!

"Postpone the concert," some of the neighbors urged. "Singing such an important one when you're not yourself is too great a risk." But Mr. Hurok had invited top critics, men whose opinions were valued throughout the country. He had paid for ads, posters, programs; postponement would cost him time and money. She decided to sing as planned.

Mr. Hurok suggested she stay at a hotel close to Town Hall when she came to New York rather than at the Y.W.C.A. in Harlem. Marian had to admit that getting around on crutches was difficult, and Hurok tried to get her a room downtown. Marian Anderson, the toast of Europe, welcomed and honored in the finest hotels on the Continent, simply wasn't wanted by one Manhattan hotel because she was Negro.

If she was hurt or upset, no one ever knew it. "Don't worry," she told Mr. Hurok, "I'll be comfortable at the Y." And that is where she stayed.

The day before the concert she took a cab to Mr. Hurok's office for a press conference. When reporters arrived, she was comfortably seated behind his desk, her cast hidden by a wastebasket. As always, she wanted to be judged for one thing only—her voice. The secret was kept. She had worked too long and hard to have judgments clouded by sympathy!

The next day, December 30, 1935, a bad snowstorm left New York icy cold. Said *Time* magazine:

> . . . From the Harlem Y.W.C.A. . . . a slender young Negro woman was lifted into a taxicab and driven away to Manhattan's Town Hall, where one of the most curious audiences of the season had gathered to hear a singer whose name had already spread the length and breadth of Europe.

Usually at a recital, the curtains are open when the audience enters the hall, and they see the artist and accompanist walk onstage and take their places. That night was different. The curtains were drawn until time for the recital to begin. At exactly eight forty-five, lights dimmed, curtains parted, and standing in the curve of the piano was the artist, her hair fashionably bobbed—beautiful, dignified, her black and gold brocaded gown flowing about her feet. Kosti and a nurse had helped her onstage with the curtains closed. The audience, completely unaware that anything was wrong, saw no telltale trace of white cast beneath her skirt, no glimmer of pain in her large, dark eyes.

Leaning lightly on the piano to keep her balance, she smiled and nodded for Kosti to begin. Closing her eyes, she forgot she was in Town Hall where she had once failed, forgot her pain, forgot everything but her music.

She sang the first tone of Handel's "Begrüssung," so difficult it's rarely sung in concert. Half a minute long was the opening tone. She sang it softly at first, then louder, louder, without a break or quaver.

Years later Howard Taubman, *The New York Times* music critic, recalled the event. "The very sound of the voice was electrifying," he said. "Full, opulent, velvety, it swelled out like a mighty organ. It moved . . . lightly over swift technical hedges as if they did not exist, always devoting itself to the flight of Handel's inspiration."

"Why start with such a difficult selection?" Mr. Hurok had asked. "Rearrange your program—"

Marian had refused.

"When you understand the how and why of singing, you will be able to perform well no matter how you feel," Boghetti had said. Apparently she now knew the how, the why. For in spite of her fractured ankle and the heavy, uncomfortable cast, she never sang better. The audience was spellbound, and not until the concert was half over did she tell them about her injury. "I am standing up," she explained simply, "to make things pleasanter for your eyes."

"The house, already adoring, burst into abandoned applause in tribute to her courage," said Mr. Hurok. "She took this calmly, too, and continued her concert with the same devoted concentration to music characteristic of her when she sings, which wins the same single-minded attention from her audience."

As for Kosti, no one in the audience seemed to object to his being white. Marian was sure that the applause was a tribute to his beautiful piano-playing as well as her singing.

One person in the audience didn't applaud at all: a small figure, dressed in black, sat quietly with her worn hands in her lap. The woman sitting next to her clapped frantically. She stopped a moment, her hands in midair. "Heavens! What's wrong with you, woman?" she asked. "Don't you know a great artist when you hear one?" Mrs. Anderson, Marian's mother, nodded and smiled.

Marian's sisters were there and Boghetti, and sitting in the third row was Orpheus "King" Fisher, still Marian's favorite admirer.

Next morning America hailed its new "high priestess of song." Wrote Critic Taubman in *The New York Times:*

> Let it be said at the outset: Marian Anderson has returned to her native land one of the great singers of our time . . . mistress of all she surveyed . . . sheer magnificence of the voice . . . contralto of stunning range and volume . . . penetrating command of style. In the last four years, Europe has acclaimed this tall, handsome girl. It is time for her own country to honor her.

The Harlem Y.W.C.A. was besieged by calls from reporters wanting to interview her and society people eager to give parties in her honor. They were all disappointed. Marian had already gone back to Philadelphia. Said *Time:*

> Most singers are all too eager to capitalize on a sure-fire success. [But] to get a glimpse of Marian Anderson after last week's concert, it was necessary to travel to Philadelphia . . . [where] the season's outstanding new singer sat with her bad foot propped up, wrapped in a clumsy gray woolen sock. . . . She could have been roundly feted if she had chosen to remain in Manhattan. . . . Instead, she preferred to hide away in her mother's Philadelphia home, with its starched lace curtains, its overstuffed furniture, its radio, its fireplace aglow with artificial flames.

Marian did accept the honors that meant most to her. By public demand she sang at jam-packed Carnegie Hall, her leg still in a cast. And with her ankle on the mend, she was off on her first tour under Hurok management.

"You're sending her out to sing with a white accompanist?" said some of Mr. Hurok's associates. "New York was one thing, but in other cities she might be stoned."

No such thing happened. "Marian sang," said Mr. Hurok, "and her audiences fell at her feet."

After a second appearance at Carnegie Hall, she returned to Europe to fulfill her commitments there, this time in the biggest, finest concert halls like Queen's Hall in London and the Paris Opera House. Before she came along, only Rachmaninoff and Kreisler had ever sold out for a solo performance at the Opera House.

"When she appeared in her Molyneux gown of gold lamé," said Kosti, "wearing a diamond brooch and topaz ring, in the golden surroundings of the Opera House, no one could believe that this statuesque woman was the same young girl who, four years previously, had cut the train off her gown because it was 'too much.'"

In Vienna she was engaged to sing the long, difficult alto solo part in Brahm's "Alto Rhapsody," under the direction of world-famous conductor, Bruno Walter. She had never sung the Rhapsody before, and the day before the concert, she held the music in her hand while rehearsing with the orchestra.

"Good-by until tomorrow," said Mr. Walter when she finished, "and Miss Anderson—when one sings under my direction, one usually does not use music."

The next evening Marian sang the part perfectly without music. She had memorized the entire part overnight! Amazed, Mr. Walter reached out and gave her hand a hearty shake.

There followed two concerts at the Salzburg Festival, Budapest, The Hague, and Barcelona, a short rest in the south of France, and off to South America.

The liner *Augustus* sailed from Cannes around the southern coast of Spain through the Straits of Gibraltar to Dakar on the West Coast of Africa. Here, there was a short stopover.

As Marian and Kosti walked through the streets of Dakar, native women in colorful robes and elaborate coiffures, stared at Marian curiously. The beautiful, dark-skinned woman, dressed in the height of European fashion looked as strange to them as they did to her. Later Marian confessed she thought their hairdos were quite elegant and their bright-colored dresses best suited to their environment.

From Dakar the ship crossed the South Atlantic to Brazil. Here Marian and Kosti did some sight-seeing between concerts, and one day they visited a world-famous snake farm. They were standing at the edge of a big basin while Marian snapped pictures of poisonous snakes and giant frogs. Suddenly one of the biggest snakes tried to escape. It wriggled halfway up, fell down, and slithered into a corner. All at once, as if in one final desperate attempt, it stood up straight. Head over the top, tail swinging, its struggles were rewarded—the snake was free.

Marian stepped back, looked the creature straight in the eye, and snapped a picture.

"She didn't seem the least afraid," said Kosti, "only tense with curiosity."

The snake lay still a moment, then wound its way toward the road. Kosti ran for the caretaker, and when the two men returned, the snake was writhing along the road, Marian close behind, snapping pictures.

The caretaker sprang forward and grabbed the snake by the neck. "*Não liberdade!*" (No freedom for you) he scolded, shaking his finger as if at a naughty child.

The snake twisted itself around the keeper's body. But he unwound it skillfully and tossed it back into the basin. Fascinated, Marian watched the weary snake wriggle to a pool and drink.

A year later Kosti met someone who had visited the same snake farm. "The caretaker," said Kosti's friend, "delights in telling tourists how one of his biggest snakes escaped—on the very day of Marian Anderson's visit."

11

B ACK in the United States came the real test: Could Marian overcome racial prejudice in the South? Mr. Hurok had scheduled her to sing over a hundred concerts in more than seventy cities. "The longest, most intensive tour of any singer in concert history," he said. And the tour included the finest halls south of the Mason-Dixon line. What would happen when she appeared onstage with Kosti, in violation of the old southern taboo? At first there was a shocked pause. Then came thunderous applause. Intelligent, fair-minded southerners were applauding her courage, as well as her voice.

While praising her art, southern newspapers, afraid of antagonizing their readers, called her "Marian Anderson," "Artist Anderson," "Singer Anderson," for in the South a Negro was rarely addressed as "Miss" or "Mr."

"Anyway," said Edwin Embree in his book *Thirteen Against the Odds*, "no reporter thought it necessary to call her 'Marian.' And the critics broke the southern stereotype by calling her beautiful and describing her clothes."

When Marian appeared in halls where Negroes had to sit apart from whites, she always bowed to her own people first, then to the rest of the audience. She did this simply with dignified humility. It seemed to be her way of telling her people and the rest of the world that she could not and would not forget she was Negro, when the world refused to let all Negroes forget.

Later, Marian insisted on "vertical seating"—that is, she asked that Negro ticket buyers, although seated apart from whites, be allotted seats in every part of the auditorium and not only in the balcony. As she became more renowned, white people were sold tickets first and the Negro section grew smaller and smaller. Marian asked that Negroes be given a chance to buy seats first come, first served. Finally she refused to appear in segregated halls.

It didn't take long for Mr. Hurok to realize his problem was not to get Marian engagements, but to decide which ones to accept. He received so many requests for Marian to appear at concerts, sing on radio, and make records that no one, he said, could meet the demand clamoring at his door. He couldn't help gloating when he met Mr. Judson, her ex-manager, in an elevator one day. "We were getting a fee of four figures that season," said Hurok, chuckling, "and though I used a slightly larger figure to impress Judson, Marian never let me down. We reached that fee the very next season."

The Hurok office did everything possible to protect Marian from embarrassment and see that she always had a comfortable place to stay. Often she stayed in private homes, and if finding her a room in a certain city was difficult, Hurok wrote the local manager. If a comfortable room convenient to the concert hall wasn't located, he said, the Hurok office would not only deprive the city of Miss Anderson's talent, they'd send none of their other clients either. Usually a room was found.

Mr. Hurok could not always shield her from unpleasant situations, and she had only to look at her itinerary to know when she was staying at a hotel generally closed to Negroes. She tried not to think about it. Singing her best was what mattered most, and if she brooded about having to stay where she wasn't wanted, how could she sing as if her heart were full of love and joy? She went to segregated hotels because she had to, and she tried to leave everyone she met at such a hotel with the feeling that prejudice was based on "insufficient knowledge," as she put it. If they discovered they had been wrong about her, perhaps they would begin to realize it was wrong to judge any group by the behavior of some. Often the people who acted coolest when she came were most cordial when she left. "We were glad to have you," they said. "Please come again."

Ironic situations often arose. Once she was paid thousands of dollars to sing two songs at the gala opening of the motion picture *Young Mr. Lincoln*, in Springfield, Illinois, but was refused a room in the city's leading hotel. Another time she was presented with the keys to Atlantic City, but could not spend the night there. Mr. Hurok was unable to protect her from the hurt when a southern committee woman drew back from her outstretched hand; the embarrassment when she and a white family at whose home she'd been staying had to use separate waiting rooms at a train station; the inconvenience when she and Kosti were refused admittance to a restaurant; the indignity of having a woman ask why she didn't sing "Chattanooga Choochoo."

Marian took such rebuffs quietly, calmly. She felt that singing was her most effective weapon against prejudice. One summer night in Jackson, Mississippi, she proved it. In ninety-degree heat she sang five encores, and not one of the four thousand people in the audience made a move to leave. Her sixth encore was "Swanee River," and she invited the audience to sing the second stanza with her. The entire assembly, Negro and white, rose as one and sang. When it was over, and cheers and applause swept the hall, she neither felt nor acted like a triumphant heroine. She was deeply moved that her audience was pleased.

"Sometimes," said the Jackson newspaper, "the human soul rises above itself, above racial prejudices."

Whether in the North or South, greeting people backstage after any concert was a thrilling experience. Masses of admirers, white and Negro, swarmed by, yearning to speak to her, shake her hand, get her autograph, or see her close. "How

101

lovely she is," they said. "So much prettier than I thought."
"What a beautiful speaking voice!" "Such a gracious lady!"
For even in the South, segregation backstage was unknown.
True, there weren't many elderly white people in that line of
admirers, but dozens of Negro and white teen-agers stood in
line together for a chance to greet her personally.

Marian's gentle nature prevented her from lashing out
against ignorant prejudice, but her colleagues were ever ready
to rise to her defense. Once on one of their trips to Washington, D.C., Kosti was invited to dine at the home of a prominent person. At his right sat a woman wearing an armful of
diamond bracelets.

"Mr. Vehanen," she said with a wry smile, "aren't you
ashamed to be the accompanist to a colored woman? Don't
you know that soon no one will invite you to their homes or
want to be in your presence?"

Kosti hesitated. His English was not too good, and he
wanted to think out his answer carefully. He replied, "Don't
you understand," he said slowly, "that your narrow thinking
makes it impossible for you to enter the doors through which
Miss Anderson goes?"

The woman's face turned red. "You can't name one place
where doors are open to her and not me," she said.

"Oh, yes I can. The doors of President and Mrs. Roosevelt's
private apartments at the White House. Miss Anderson has
been invited to sing there next week." Kosti turned to speak
to the guest on his left.

In 1936, Marian sang at the White House for the first
time, and Mrs. Roosevelt graciously invited Marian's mother.
As they entered the music room, President Roosevelt looked
up from the big, comfortable sofa beside a roaring fire, smiled
broadly, and said: "Why, hello, there, Miss Anderson. You
look just like your photographs, don't you?"

That was one of the few times in her career Marian ever
felt flustered. She was so tongue-tied she couldn't recite the
little speech she had prepared. But the President's friendly

handshake and warm welcome made her feel completely at ease again.

When she finished singing, Mrs. Roosevelt put the crowning touch on the occasion. Taking Mama by the hand, she led her across the room and introduced her to the President!

12

C OULD this be the same inexperienced traveler who, eight years before, had lost her music case in a London railroad station? Marian took such an assortment of things on her travels now, she usually needed two taxis, one for herself and her accompanist, one for her luggage. She took an electric hot plate, pans, and dishes, for she preferred to prepare her meals in her room; a sewing machine to make slacks for herself or a blouse for her mother; a phonograph; a tape recorder; a radio; a sleeping bag for naps on cold trains; an electric iron —all this and her wardrobe too.

As with anyone in the public eye, clothes were important, especially evening gowns or "working clothes," as she called them. Most singers took a maid on tour with them. Marian preferred to do things herself. A typical scene in a hotel room before a concert would find Marian pressing a gown over a big suitcase padded with newspapers and towels, while her supper simmered on a hot plate.

Most of Marian's gowns were created especially for her by Parisian, Viennese, or fine American designers. Well-made gowns of good materials not only looked better onstage but lasted longer, and her own people, especially those in the South, took particular pride in seeing her well dressed. "I owe it to the public to look the best I can," she once said, "and no one need tell me I'm not a glamor girl."

Perhaps she wasn't in the usual sense. But, wrote Marcia

Davenport in an article in *Collier's* magazine, when Marian Anderson, mistress of her art, stands on a stage beautifully dressed in quiet white or elegant brocade, she is one of the proudest ornaments her country ever had.

Evidently not everyone thought so. For in that year 1939, when Hitler was trying to squash freedom in Europe, the D.A.R. (Daughters of the American Revolution), descendants of men who had given their lives to build a nation where all men are created equal, refused to let Marian Anderson sing at Constitution Hall, in Washington, D.C.

Marian was besieged by reporters. "How do you feel about it?" she was asked at train stations, in front of concert halls, outside hotels.

Marian felt only sadness. It started in June, 1938, when the Hurok office received a routine request from Howard University, asking for a Marian Anderson concert. Hurok named a date, April 9, 1939, and a reservation was requested at Constitution Hall, the only large auditorium in Washington.

Sorry, replied officers of the D.A.R., owners of the hall, it was taken for that date. Hurok suggested others. *All* dates were taken, replied the D.A.R. Investigation showed that a clause in the rental contract prohibited Negroes from appearing there.

The world was shocked. Leading musicians whom Marian did not know canceled their concerts at Constitution Hall; journalists, government and religious leaders, public and private citizens alike, rose as one. This insult to American democracy was more than they could stand.

"I am ashamed to play at Constitution Hall," said Jasha Heifitz, one of the world's leading violinists.

"One of the most monstrous and stupid things that has happened in America in years," said Heywood Broun, journalist.

Walter Damrosch, composer-conductor; Deems Taylor, critic; Lawrence Tibbett, Metropolitan star and president of the American Guild of Musical Artists; Fiorello La Guardia, Mayor of New York City; and hundreds of others sent the D.A.R. wires of protest. Wired Deems Taylor:

This action subverts the clear meaning of the U.S. Constitution, in particular the Bill of Rights, and places your organization in the camp of those who seek to destroy democracy, justice, and liberty.

Then came the climax: In her syndicated newspaper column "My Day," Eleanor Roosevelt announced her resignation from the D.A.R. Newspapers over the country headlined her resignation, and a wave of others followed. Mrs. Giuseppe Boghetti; Josephine Truslow Adams, of the Massachusetts Adamses; Dr. Elsie Mitchell, of California. Others set up their own D.A.R. with a policy of nondiscrimination. Furthermore, some local chapters of the D.A.R. objected to Washington's action. This, Marian said later, confirmed her opinion that a whole group must not be condemned for the actions of a few.

Not everyone sympathized with Marian. Columnist Westbrook Pegler called her a "hitherto obscure Negro singer," and hinted that the whole affair was a publicity stunt. "An obscure singer"—after Salzburg, L'Opera de Paris, the White House, Carnegie Hall, and winning the Grand Prix du Chant for the best recorded voice in Europe!

"Perhaps," said Mr. Hurok, "Mr. Pegler was trying to be funny."

This was no publicity stunt; but a spontaneous uprising of people of goodwill. "This is America," they were saying to the rest of the world, "not Nazi Germany." And the world watched with interest. Parisian newspapers, for example, devoted long columns to the affair.

Meanwhile Howard University, more eager than ever for a Marian Anderson concert, asked the Washington, D.C., Board of Education for the use of the auditorium at Central High School. The request was denied. Over a thousand indignant citizens formed a protest committee, picketed the board's office, and sent them a petition with thousands of signatures. The request was still denied. The high school students themselves wrote an editorial for their school paper:

> Let us hope that it [the Board] does reconsider and do Central the honor of playing host to one of the musical world's greatest artists, as well as prove to the rest of the world that this country holds no grudges because of race or color.

The principal of Central High, unwilling to have the students criticize their Board of Education, suppressed the editorial before it was published.

On February 24, Mr. Hurok made an announcement. Marian Anderson *would* sing in Washington, D.C. She would sing out-of-doors within earshot of the D.A.R.'s Constitution Hall. At the invitation of the United States Department of the Interior, she would sing an Easter Sunday Concert at the Lincoln Memorial.

Marian consented reluctantly. The idea of the concert was good, but the furor of the whole affair upset her quiet nature, and the night before Easter she phoned Mr. Hurok from Philadelphia. "Must we go through with it?" she asked. On the eve of her greatest concert, Marian was frightened.

Yes, they must, said Mr. Hurok. Marian Anderson, the individual, was unimportant now. Whether she wanted to or not, and she did not, she had become a symbol of her race.

Easter Sunday dawned cloudy, gray. Busy bellhops all over Washington murmured the same prayer: "Please don't let it rain."

Mr. Hurok met Marian and her mother at the station. While police sirens shrieked, he drove them to the home of the former governor of Pennsylvania, Gifford Pinchot, where they would remain until concert time.

Among the official greeters was Olive Ewing Clapper, wife of Raymond Clapper, the Washington correspondent. Mrs.

107

Clapper described the incident in her book *Washington Tapestry*.

"Hello, Miss Anderson," she said as Marian got out of the car. "How are you?"

"Oh, Mrs. Clapper, I've never been so frightened in my life! I don't see how I can possibly sing."

Mrs. Clapper took her hand. "I have a message for you from my sixteen-year-old daughter," she said. "Tell Miss Anderson not to be worried or frightened—to relax, and let her glorious voice roll out to us in all its beauty."

"Thank you very much," said Marian. "That was all I needed. I'll be all right now." She went upstairs to rest, change, and go over her music. When she came down, she was dressed in a long black velvet gown, and Mr. Hurok handed her an orchid to pin on her shoulder. She pinned it on her mother instead.

They drove to Lincoln Memorial, again escorted by police. The past few days had been filled with rumors, even threats against Marian's personal safety. "But as Marian walked beside me along the roped-off aisle and up the steps to the platform, where great men and women of America stood to honor her," said Mr. Hurok, "the arm which I took to steady her was steadier than my own."

The bellhops' prayers had been answered. The sky was blue, and the sun shone down on blossoming cherry trees and soft spring grass. Congressmen, some born in the South, were there. Also present were Supreme Court Justices, Secretary of the Treasury Morgenthau, and dozens of other dignitaries. Secretary of the Interior Harold Ickes made the introduction:

"In this great auditorium under the sky all of us are free. When God gave us this wonderful outdoors and the sun and the moon and the stars, he made no distinction of race or creed or color. And one hundred and thirty years ago he sent to us one of his truly great in order that he might restore freedom to those from whom we had disregardfully taken it. In carrying out this task, Abraham Lincoln laid down his life, and so it is appropriate as it is fortunate that today we stand reverently and humbly at the base of this memorial to the Great Emancipator while glorious tribute is rendered his memory by a daughter of the race from which he struck the chains of slavery.

"Facing us down the Mall beyond the Washington Monument, which we have erected as a symbol of the towering stature and fame of him who founded this Republic, there is rising a memorial to that other great democrat in our short history, Thomas Jefferson, who proclaimed that principle of equality of opportunity which Abraham Lincoln believed in so implicitly, and took so seriously. In our own time, too many pay mere lip service to these twin planets in our democratic heaven. There are some, even in this great Capital of our great democratic Republic, who are either too timid or too indifferent to lift up the light that Jefferson and Lincoln carried aloft.

"Genius, like justice, is blind. For genius has touched with the tip of her wing this woman who, if it had not been for the great mind of Lincoln, would not be able to stand among us today a free individual in a free land. Genius draws no color line. She has endowed Marian Anderson with such a voice as lifts any individual above his fellows, as is a matter of exultant pride to any race. And so it is fitting that Marian Anderson should raise her voice in tribute to the noble Lincoln, whom mankind will ever honor.

"We are grateful to Miss Marian Anderson for coming here to sing for us today."

Marian, regal, dignified, her fur coat around her shoulders, moved between the marble columns of the Memorial and stood before the great sculptured figure of Lincoln. She looked out over the crowd. There were people as far as she could see, around the mirror pool, up the Mall far to the east, toward Washington Monument. Seventy-five thousand people, men, women, children, Negro and white, stood side by side, faces upturned, eyes, ears, and hearts fixed on her.

Together they sang "The Star-spangled Banner."

109

When Marian, with Lincoln looking over her shoulder, had sung the "Ave Maria," an operatic aria, and spirituals of her people, the shouting would not die down.

"I am overwhelmed," she said simply. "I can't tell you what you have done for me today. I thank you from the bottom of my heart again and again."

On Easter Sunday, 1939, Marian Anderson sang at the Lincoln Memorial in Washington, D.C.

Years later in this country and abroad people still came backstage especially to tell her they had been there. In 1943 a mural commemorating the historic event for future generations was painted on the wall of the Department of Interior in Washington. "Marian Anderson's voice and personality have come to be a symbol of the willing acceptance of the immortal truth that 'all men are created free and equal,'" said Secretary Ickes at the unveiling of the mural.

Marian was to make a speech then, and newsreel men, afraid she might hesitate for a word, suggested she read it. That was unnecessary. The words came from her heart. "I am deeply touched," she said, "that I can be in any way a symbol of democracy. Everyone present was a living witness to the ideals of freedom for which President Lincoln died. When I sang that day, I was singing to the entire nation."

The evening after the unveiling of the mural, Marian sang at a benefit for China Relief at Constitution Hall by invitation of the D.A.R. Later, the anti-Negro clause was struck out of the rental agreement, and she sang there regularly.

"When I finally walked onto the stage of Constitution Hall," she said, "I felt no different than I had in other halls. There was no sense of triumph. I felt that it was a beautiful concert hall and I was very happy to sing there."

A few weeks after that unforgettable Easter Sunday, Marian was asked to sing at the White House again, this time before King George VI and Queen Elizabeth of England. Afterward she and the other performers, Kate Smith, Lawrence Tibbett, and cowboy-folk singer Alan Lomax, were presented to the King and Queen.

Marian curtsied to the Queen, but not very well, she admitted later. Moving down the receiving line, she greeted Mrs. Roosevelt. Next came the King. Afraid to risk another curtsy, Marian decided to shake hands with him instead. Later she realized she had done neither. In her excitement she had passed the King of England without so much as a how do you do!

Mrs. Anna Anderson posed with her daughter following the Easter concert at the Lincoln Memorial.

Miss Anderson received the Spingarn Medal in July, 1939. Mrs. Franklin Delano Roosevelt presented her with the citation.

That was in June, 1939. In July another honor—the Spingarn Medal, given by the NAACP (National Association for the Advancement of Colored People) to the American Negro achieving most during the year. Mrs. Roosevelt presented the citation:

"Marian Anderson has been chosen for her special achievement in the field of music. Equally with that achievement, which has won her worldwide fame as one of the greatest singers of our time, is her magnificent dignity as a human being. Her unassuming manner, which has not been changed by her phenomenal success, has added to the esteem not only of Marian Anderson as an individual, but of the race to which she belongs."

Her nation and her own people honored her; so did the city in which she was born. On March 18, 1941, Marian was given

113

Her mother was also present when she received the Bok Award on March 18, 1941.

the Bok Award, presented annually to the citizen of which Philadelphia is proudest. She was the first Negro and the second woman to receive the award. The first woman was Dr. Lucy Langdon Wilson, the high school principal who had introduced her to Mr. Boghetti!

"That this honor should come to me," said Marian, "was not in my wildest dreams," and she earmarked the ten-

The 1941 Toronto Flower Show
was visited by Marian Anderson.

thousand-dollar award as the basis of a scholarship[2] to be presented to worthy music students regardless of race. When the original ten thousand dollars ran out, she replenished it, and by 1964 more than eighty young musicians of all races had received scholarships amounting to over forty thousand dollars. Some of the prize winners, like Mattiwilda Dobbs, Camilla Williams, and Grace Bumbry, became famous themselves.

During World War II, Marian toured the United States, singing for the Armed Forces in camps and hospitals. Servicemen were as enthralled with her music as audiences in the finest concert halls. When she sang for badly wounded men in a Kansas hospital, for instance, doctors asked that she sing only fifteen minutes or the men might become restless. Later the doctors admitted they had been wrong. When the fifteen minutes were up, the patients begged her to sing more.

War workers enjoyed her music. After she had christened the *Booker T. Washington* ship, workers in a California shipyard perched on scaffolds and riggings, listening to her sing, cheering her on to encore after encore.

---

[2] For information about the scholarship, write: Marian Anderson Scholarship Fund, 762 South Martin Street, Philadelphia, Pa. 19146.

115

WHENEVER she was in Philadelphia, Marian stayed with her mother in the house on South Martin Street. She went to the Union Baptist Church. She took lessons from Mr. Boghetti, and *he* still said, "Neither man nor contralto was meant to live alone."

In July of 1943, in a Connecticut church, Marian married her best beau—Orpheus "King" Fisher, now a prominent architect.

"Marriage to King was worth waiting for," she said simply, and she liked to tell how, when they first got home, she overheard King say to the servants: "The first one who calls my wife 'Marian Anderson' gets discharged!" Years later, however, when someone phoned and asked if Mrs. Fisher was home, he said: "I'm sorry, my wife, Marian Anderson, is at

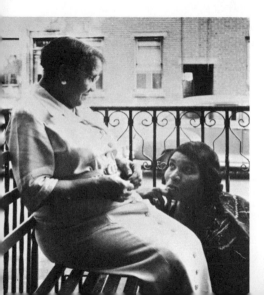

Miss Anderson and her mother at the family home in South Philadelphia.

the recording studio." For King loved Mrs. Fisher, but like the rest of the world, he was proud of Marian Anderson!

Mr. and Mrs. Fisher bought a big farmhouse surrounded by acres of lovely countryside near Danbury, Connecticut. Sometimes King traveled with her, but more often his own business kept him in New York and Connecticut. Their summers and weekends together were all the more precious because of the time they had been apart.

How Marian loved to go home to Marianna Farm after long hours on trains, planes, or in cold, impersonal hotel rooms! Mama and her sisters visited for weeks at a time, and now there was an addition to Marian's "little family," as she called it. It was Ethel's small son, Jimmy, who helped his Aunt Marian collect eggs from the hens, plant beans in the garden, feed the chickens, cows, horses, and pigs.

At the farm in Danbury, Connecticut.

Dogs find a happy home with Marian Anderson on the Danbury farm.

Marian loved animals, and she was always careful not to frighten or disturb them. Before entering the chicken house, she opened the door and peeked inside; she approached the cows slowly, speaking to them in soft, gentle tones. At one time, prize black Angus steer were raised on the farm, but they proved economically unsound. Marian refused to eat them.

Cats and dogs were always about, usually Airedales, or Kerry Blue Terriers. And when Marian adopted a little black kitten from the cat family living in the barn, her friend, writer-composer Frida Sarsen-Bucky, was inspired to write words and music for a children's record called *Snoopy Cat*. In it Marian tells how Snoopy burns her paw in hot soup, falls into a flour bin, hides in Marian's suitcase, and wanders onstage in the middle of a concert.

"The record is a delight," said *The New York Times*. "Miss Anderson tells of her cat, Snoopy, with intense warmth, in a slow, carefully cadenced voice, and sings of her with true power and beauty."

Marian set aside some of her time at home for practice. On tour she didn't work on her voice nearly as much as she liked. For whether she was staying in a hotel or a private home, she was always afraid of "disturbing the neighbors." On the farm she could practice as much as she liked without disturbing anyone. King designed and built a separate studio for her, a short walk from the house. It was complete with recording

Many hours are spent in this studio at her farm.

and sound equipment. Here Marian practiced in front of a big window overlooking the brook that King had dammed up, to make a rustic "swimming hole."

Kosti had returned to Finland, and Marian had a new accompanist, Franz Rupp, a fine musician who had escaped from the Nazis. Before each new season, Franz and his wife, Steffi, came to the farm and stayed in the guesthouse. After Mr. Boghetti's death, Steffi became Marian's vocal coach.

To Marian, selecting music for her programs was like choosing what to wear from a large wardrobe. "If a woman has a blue dress and a black one, she has no trouble. If she has fifty dresses, she has a problem."

Because she'd been learning new songs through the years, Marian had a problem. She always tried to plan her programs with all her listeners in mind. There were those who were naturally musical or had studied music, and those who had no musical background but came to her concerts to be entertained. Occasionally she was surprised. For example, when she sang for war workers, she expected them to ask for light music, but they often requested more serious pieces.

Marian selected the music for the next season at the beginning of each summer. First she went through seven volumes of Schubert, the composer she liked best. Schubert had written hundreds of songs, each one seeming lovelier than the other, and before long she had chosen enough to fill a whole program. Audiences wanted to hear other composers' music as well, so she considered Brahms, Schumann, Wolf, Strauss, and French, Spanish, Italian, and English composers. Every year she tried to sing at least one new song by an unknown American composer, and she always included a group of Negro spirituals. "They are the unburdening of the sorrows of an entire race which, finding scant happiness on earth, turns to the future for its joy," she said.

Once the new songs for a program were selected, she set about learning each one. First she listened to the melody. Then she read the words and tried to understand their deep-

120

est meaning. She looked up the composer's life to find out what kind of person he was, how he happened to write that particular song, and when she put words and music together, she tried to create the exact mood the composer had intended. With Franz at the piano, she sang each new song into her tape recorder and played it back, listening to herself with a sharp ear for improvement. "I want my listeners to forget Marian Anderson," she said, "and think only of the composer and his music."

But it wasn't always easy to study, even with her wonderful new studio. Her home, family, and outside obligations were often on her mind, and no matter how much she worked during the day she continued to study her music before she went to sleep as she had when she had first started taking lessons from Boghetti.

Many people were curious about Marian's voice, which was often called a *pair* of voices: the upper half, brilliant, flexible, actually soprano; the lower half, thrillingly deep. Critics often marveled at the way she switched from "one" voice to the "other," with no trouble. Once in Brazil, two distinguished-looking doctors came backstage to see her during intermission. She didn't understand Portuguese, but she finally figured out that they wanted to look down her throat. She wondered why. She felt all right. Perhaps it was a Brazilian custom. She opened her mouth, the gentlemen stared inside, talked to each other, bowed to her, and walked out. She never did learn what they were looking for, or if they thought they had found it!

But the lady with the voice that made doctors curious was Marian Anderson. The other Marian, Mrs. Orpheus Fisher, wasn't too different from other housewives. She enjoyed keeping house, and didn't mind wielding a broom or dust-cloth. "I know how to use a mop, hot water, and soap," she said proudly, thinking perhaps of the steps she'd scrubbed as a child in Philadelphia. She canned vegetables from her gar-

121

den, shopped for bargains at discount fabric stores, made drapes and slipcovers, upholstered chairs and refinished tables she'd bought at roadside antique shops. And one summer the slacks she made at a local dressmaking class earned the Voice of a Century yet another title: The Denim Belle of Fairfield County. She was leaving Danbury's tiny post office one day when a local citizen pointed her out to a visitor.

"*That's* Marian Anderson?" she overheard the visitor say incredulously. "It can't be—she's wearing sneakers!"

Marian and King did not often plan formal entertaining or elaborate parties. They spent quiet evenings at home playing with their dogs and cats, listening to the radio or watching television; and occasionally King would sing while she accompanied him on the piano. Before her marriage Marian had many acquaintances, people who came backstage after concerts or entertained her in their homes when she traveled, but her circle of close friends was small. Kosti used to call her heart a little golden casket that was hard to open. But, he continued, anyone who got to know her well found an exquisite pearl in the casket, carefully guarded so as not to disturb the serenity of her soul.

Gradually, however, Marian began to form deep friendships, both Negro and white, and she and King had many friends in common, such as author Rex Stout and his wife, who lived close by and often came over to spend an evening listening to Marian's collection of records, the composer Frida Sarson-Bucky, Sophia Jacobs, the author Emily Kimbrough, Dr. and Mrs. Sylvester Carter, Mr. and Mrs. Alonzo Browne, Mr. and Mrs. James Owens, Mr. and Mrs. Hobson Reynolds.

Marian's beloved farm was not acquired without heartache. Before they decided on Marianna, she and King tried to buy many others. It wasn't hard to figure out why prices kept soaring. "One of the strange things about it," said Marian, "was that King could live anywhere he chose if he weren't married to me." For, though he was Negro, King had a very

122

light skin and was often taken for white. For a few years before they were married, he had "passed" as white to prove himself in his profession. Like other Negroes compelled to "pass" to prove their worth and support their families, King hated the deception and gave it up.

Eventually Marian and King sold the original farmhouse and built a contemporary ranch on the same grounds. King designed the house with huge picture windows overlooking the valley below, a great flagstone fireplace in the living room, and enormous closets with specially high rods for his wife's concert gowns. "I don't see how we can build a house around your evening clothes," he had once said jokingly. But he did manage to find a way to do it.

Miss Anderson and her husband, Orpheus Fisher, enjoy riding horseback through the Connecticut countryside.

123

Later a room in the new house became his office. When Marian peeked over his shoulder from time to time as he drew up architectural plans for his clients, he taught her how to read a blueprint. "I wouldn't want people to think the wife of an architect doesn't understand these things!" Marian's husband said.

With Marian traveling so much, decorating and furnishing their home took a long time. She decided to make curtains while she was on tour. King laughed and bet her five dollars she wouldn't finish them before she got home. Finish them she did, hems, linings, and pleats!

Often when she arrived in a city, a package would be waiting for her—wallpaper samples or swatches of slipcover fabric that King had mailed for her approval. Between concerts she shopped for her home. In Hawaii she bought rattan furniture for her studio; in Sweden she bought glasses; in Denmark, porcelain; in Norway, enamelware; and in Finland, dishes. She brought home interesting seeds for her garden from foreign countries, exotic spices, herbs, and most of all, recipes. King was game to try anything—sweet and sour shrimp, French style; Swedish wild duck; and authentic Chinese food.

One day in Chicago, Marian was having lunch in her hotel room, when a demonstrator on TV showed how to make a new kind of pudding. Cleverly he gave half the recipe, suggesting that the viewer buy his cookbook for the rest. Marian went right out and bought the book. She could hardly wait to get home to try the recipe.

But Marian's cooking was not always successful, especially when music was on her mind. One summer a British manager named Mr. Hill visited the farm on short notice. The girl who helped Marian with housework was off that day, so Marian made the preparations herself. She phoned the butcher early in the morning and ordered a roast of beef. Then she went down to the studio and became absorbed in music. When she returned to the house, the roast hadn't arrived. She called the butcher. He replied that he was sorry but there was no one

124

to deliver it. After another hour's work with Franz, she drove into town herself for the meat. When she returned, she consulted her cookbook and prepared the meat according to directions. She put it in the oven, set the vegetables on the stove, and went down to the studio again.

Alas—when Mr. Hill arrived, the meat was overcooked, the vegetables undercooked, the potatoes hard inside.

"That wasn't very good, was it, dear?" she asked King when dinner was over.

"No, darling. But you get 'A' for effort."

The laughter finally subsided.

"Just think," said Mr. Hill, "I can tell my grandchildren Marian Anderson prepared a whole meal for me."

"Please don't tell them what kind," Marian pleaded.

Now when she was in New York, Marian stayed at the Algonquin Hotel. Later she and King took their own apartment on Fifth Avenue across from Central Park. In spite of her fame, there were daily hurts and inconveniences, the salesgirl who turned away, the taxi driver who didn't stop, some people's overkindness, which was often more embarrassing than a snub. That was in the North. In the South there were deeper hurts and embarrassments.

The incidents were many. One in particular remained in her memory. In a certain city in the South, she, Franz Rupp, and Isaac Jofe, the traveling manager assigned her by the Hurok office, were greeted at the station by a woman they had never seen before.

"How do you do, Mr. Jofe," the woman said. "How do you do, Mr. Rupp. Hello, Marian. I'm Mrs. Davis.[3] I'm in charge of your concert here."

"How do you do, Mrs. Davis," said Marian.

"Marian, you're going to stay with a nice private family. They have a clean house, and you'll like it there." Mrs. Davis

---

[3] Not her real name.

turned to Franz and Jofe, as Marian called him. "Gentlemen, your rooms are waiting for you at the hotel. I'll take you first. Then I'll take Marian—"

"I insist upon seeing Miss Anderson's accommodations," said Jofe.

"Oh. Well, all right." Mrs. Davis drove them into the Negro section of the city.

Marian leaned forward, looking out of the car window at the crowded streets, poor-looking houses, and children playing on sidewalks.

"Marian," Mrs. Davis piped up from the front seat, "your people just love it here. They're happier here than anywhere else." She turned to Franz beside her on the front seat. "Mr. Rupp," she said, "I was just telling Marian how much better off the Nigrahs are down here, where we love them and take care of them."

Marian couldn't see Franz's face, but she could imagine his expression.

Mrs. Davis was right about one thing. The Negro family Marian stayed with was charming. She got a good night's sleep, and next morning she arrived at the auditorium for rehearsal, feeling cheerful and rested. Franz was waiting by the entrance, and they went inside together. Jofe was onstage, talking with Mrs. Davis. For some reason, he seemed upset. But he didn't say why, and she didn't ask. If he wanted to tell her, he would. After rehearsal she, Jofe, and Franz went outside to get a taxi.

They were standing by the curb when Jofe suddenly turned to Franz. "Franz," he said, "please go back and speak to that Mrs.—Mrs. Davis. I'll stay here with Marian and get her a cab."

Marian started to say it wasn't necessary, that she could get a cab herself. But she knew she probably couldn't. It was most unlikely that a driver here in the South would stop for her alone. It was odd to realize that Franz was from Germany, and Jofe from Russia, and that she was the only one from the

126

group in her native land, yet she needed them to hail a taxi for her—a woman born in Philadelphia.

That night both Franz and Jofe seemed quite nervous. When the first group of songs was over, she and Franz left the stage for a few moments' rest. The applause was overwhelming. As always, she took his hand and led him back onstage for a bow. A hush fell over the audience. Then there came a roar of applause, louder than before.

"Franz, Jofe," she said, as they took her home afterward, "what's been going on? Why were you so nervous before the concert, Jofe, and why did you go back into the hall this morning, Franz?"

"I shall tell you now," said Jofe. "When you came to the hall for rehearsal this morning, that—that woman, Mrs. Davis, was telling me she'd heard that in other cities you held your accompanist's hand when you came onstage for a bow. She wanted me to tell you that if you stood onstage holding a white man's hand, she wouldn't be responsible for what happened. I was furious, and told her what you did was your own affair. But later, I got to thinking that Franz should at least know what she'd said, so I asked him to go back so she could tell him herself."

"I told her I wouldn't pay the slightest attention to anything so ridiculous," said Franz.

"I see." Marian was quiet a moment. "Well, you see, Mrs. Davis was wrong. Nothing happened. The audience seemed to enjoy the concert very much." And she changed the subject.

"There was a time when we were very much interested in applause, and the lovely things they [the audience] said," Marian admitted to reporters one day, "but now we are interested only in singing so that the audience will depart feeling a little better than when it came."

The letters she received showed she had succeeded in the concert hall and also through her records. A woman who had lost a loved one wrote: "I just want you to know I was feeling

127

very badly when I heard some of your records, and they helped me."

Another woman sent Marian a lovely feather fan "because," she wrote, "your singing meant so much to my son during the last days of his life."

Through the years, Marian received many kinds of letters. There were letters from young singers asking for advice and from older singers who felt qualified, but never had the right opportunity. "You had your break," ended one such letter, "now give me mine."

Many of the letters asked for money for various purposes, some sad, some amusing. "Please send me twenty thousand dollars," wrote one lady from Denmark. "I intend to open a flower shop in your honor. I shall call it 'Marian'—it will be good publicity for you."

Sometimes Marian's sister Alyce handled her correspondence, and later, when it became too heavy, Marian engaged a part-time stenographer.

Marian never ceased to be amazed at things people gave her.

"To think that anyone would pay to come to my concerts," she said, "then take the trouble to bring or send me a gift!"

There was the Canadian woman who came to the hall against doctor's orders and brought a doll she'd made with her own hands; and the woman who sent her a lovely old pin with a note: "This has little monetary value, but it was my mother's favorite piece of jewelry, and I would like you to have it for your mother." Marian's home in Connecticut and her apartment in New York were filled with mementos, and she cherished every one, from the carved figure of an ancient Japanese actor, given her by the Empress of Japan, to the dainty handkerchief lovingly embroidered by an old lady from Indiana, whom she'd never seen.

Marian Anderson is America's foremost radio singer for the sixth year, said *Musical America*, after conducting a poll in 1946. In spring of 1947 she began her first tour of Jamaica and the West Indies. There were more cheers and more applause. In July of 1948 she underwent a serious operation to remove a cyst from her throat. "A very delicate matter," doctors called the operation, "a chance of permanent injury to her vocal cords."

"Her voice is like a Stradivarius in the hands of a Heifitz," Critic David Ewen had said. Would she lose it now?

Marian's faith did not waver. The good Lord had given her a voice. He would decide if she should keep it. By August she was singing again, and in October she was off on a full-scale tour of the country. In spring, 1949, she returned to Europe for the first tour in ten years, and in 1953 she toured South America and Japan.

"There must be an important person on board," she said to Franz when she saw the big crowd waiting for the plane at the Tokyo Airport.

There was. Marian Anderson. It never occurred to her that so many people were waiting to greet her.

Next day she learned that Mrs. Eleanor Roosevelt was in Tokyo, and would soon arrive at the same hotel. She was about to enter the hotel florist shop to buy Mrs. Roosevelt a welcoming corsage when she heard, "Marian Anderson! What are you doing here?" It was Mrs. Roosevelt. She had arrived ahead of time.

For a moment Marian stared at her friend, speechless. The corsage on her mind, she felt as if she'd been "caught in the act." She recovered her composure. "I'm here on a concert tour—"

Mrs. Roosevelt's face lighted up. "Are you singing in Tokyo?"

"Yes, tonight."

Mrs. Roosevelt turned to her Japanese hosts. "Is it too late?" she asked. "May I hear Marian Anderson tonight?" Mrs. Roosevelt's busy schedule was rearranged so she could.

From Tokyo, Marian went on to Kyoto, the Imperial capital, to sing at the Royal Palace and receive the Yukosho Medal

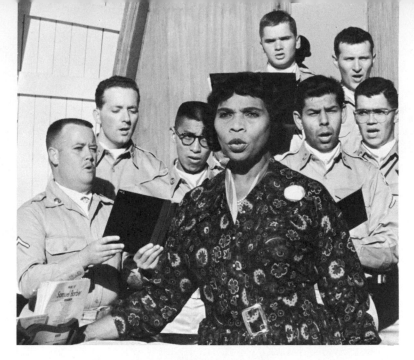

The chorus of the 24th Infantry Division sang with
Marian Anderson in Korea in 1957.

from Emperor Hirohito. After Japan she toured South Korea
to sing for servicemen in hospitals and Army camps. One of
the camps had an old-fashioned pump organ instead of a piano,
and when the performance was over, Franz Rupp remarked
that he'd just "walked ten miles."

"That's nothing," said a soldier waiting for Marian's autograph. "I went A.W.O.L. from the front to hear Miss Anderson. I've got to get back before I'm missed!" Marian gave
him the autograph at once, though she knew he was joking.

When she returned to America, Marian's native city of
Philadelphia honored her again. On a hot summer day, much
like the day she had been turned down at music school because
she was Negro, Mayor Joseph Clark dedicated the Marian
Anderson Recreation Center, swimming pool, auditorium,
gymnasium, and playground at Seventeenth and Fitzwater
Streets, in the neighborhood where she was born.

14

MARIAN had come a long way since those early days in the church choir. She had sung on almost every continent in the world, for kings and presidents, for mighty and humble. She had, however, never sung in opera. "The concert stage is better for you," Mr. Boghetti used to say. Although many years had passed, his reason was valid—a Negro had never sung with the Metropolitan Opera Company. It had been years since Stanislavski had asked her to play Carmen, and now he was dead. European opera companies had offered her parts, but it seemed as if she were waiting to sing opera in her own country. The chances for that seemed slim indeed.

One fall evening in 1954 she and King went to the opening of an English opera company in New York. Mr. Hurok had invited them to a party after the performance. Marian wasn't fond of big parties, and she decided not to go.

"It was nice of Mr. Hurok to invite us," she said to King as they left the Opera House, "but he'll have lots of other guests to worry about. Let's go home and phone our apologies."

"All right," said King amiably, "if that's what you want."

They got into their car and started for their New York apartment. A few minutes later she turned to her husband and said, "King, I've a strange feeling we should go to the party for a little while, just to say hello. Then we'll leave." King turned the car around.

The party was a dazzling affair. The cast of the opera, members of the press, and many well-known musicians were there. Marian and King were chatting with some people they knew, when a tall, thin man made his way across the crowded room and drew Marian aside. He was Rudolf Bing, manager of the Metropolitan Opera Association. "Miss Anderson," he asked casually, "would you be interested in singing with the Metropolitan?"

Her eyes widened.

"*Would* you?"

She could tell by his tone that he was serious. "Yes," she said. "I would."

"Good. Will you phone me in the morning?"

"I certainly will."

The role Mr. Bing had in mind was Ulrica, the Negro sorceress in Verdi's opera *The Masked Ball*. It was a short part but a dramatic one, and it called for a vibrant personality as well as a beautiful voice. Marian had never seen that particular opera, and when she first looked at the score, she thought the part too high for her voice. Nevertheless, she agreed to study it and audition for the music director, Dimitri Mitropoulos.

On the morning of her audition, she told him she thought the part too high for her range.

"Please sing it through," he said. "We'll see."

Marian sang, "not at all happy with the results," she said later. When she was younger, the high *a* in Ulrica's aria would have been no problem. Now she had to admit it was difficult.

Mr. Mitropoulos was encouraging. "You haven't worked on it enough yet," he said. "It will go better when you know it thoroughly."

Marian wasn't convinced, but she promised she would study the part some more and audition again. When she got back to her apartment, however, the phone was ringing.

It was Franz. "Marian!" he said excitedly. "Where have you been?"

"On the way home from the audition—"

"Mr. Hurok's been trying like mad to reach you—"

132

"Oh? What for?"

"I don't know. But he wants you to call him at once."

"All right. Thank you, Franz." She hung up and called Mr. Hurok.

"Congratulations!" he said.

"Beg your pardon?"

"Congratulations!"

"What for?"

"You got the part. You are now a member of the Metropolitan Opera Company." Marian sat down. She'd thought she was to audition again, before Mr. Mitropoulos made up his mind. He was a fine musician, and if he believed she could do it, she owed it to him and everyone else who had confidence in her to give it a try. She called her mother in Philadelphia and told her the news. She called King. She called the Rupps. And for the first time she realized, herself, how much she had wanted the part.

That afternoon she went to the Opera House to sign her contract.

"Welcome, Miss Anderson," said one of the stagehands. "Welcome home."

The next day newspapers throughout the country made the historic announcement that for the first time since its opening in 1883, a Negro would sing with the Metropolitan Opera Company.

"Does this mean other Negro singers will be welcome too?" Mr. Bing was asked.

"That would depend on whether or not the singer was right for the role," Mr. Bing replied. "I wouldn't hire anyone because he is Negro. Nor would I refuse to hire anyone for that reason."

It was obvious, though, that another bar to Negroes had been lowered. But an editorial in *The New York Times* played down the prejudice angle in favor of the singer herself. "That Marian Anderson has fulfilled a lifelong ambition is not nearly as important as the fact that we have another opportunity to hear her in still another medium," said the *Times*. "When there has been discrimination against Marian Anderson, the suffering was not hers, but ours. It was we who were impoverished, not she."

Now the real work began: hours of study with vocal coach Steffi Rupp, and hours more with operatic coaches Paul Meyer and Victor Trucco to make sure she understood the meaning of the Italian words and the proper tempo and phrasing. Then came hours more with stage director Herbert Graf in charge of acting. "Mr. Graf didn't try to turn me into an actress overnight," said Marian. "And whenever he made a suggestion, he always added: 'Do the thing that seems most natural to you.'"

Next, singing and acting were combined in sessions at the piano, followed by rehearsals with soprano Zinka Milanov and tenor Richard Tucker. Finally in late December the chorus, orchestra, and everyone else in the act assembled for the first full rehearsal onstage.

"Ready, please," called Mr. Graf. "Miss Anderson—front and center."

Marian set aside her score, mounted the dais, and began to stir the "magic brew" in a big iron caldron decorated with macabre skulls made of papier-mâché. The orchestra began to play. She took a breath, but before she could sing a note, flashbulbs popped.

Mr. Mitropoulos stopped the music. Mr. Graf folded his arms. His assistants, people in the chorus, and musicians waited and watched.

"Smile, Miss Anderson. Good. Look over here, please. Just one more." Photographers stepped aside, but only to make room for reporters.

"Are you happy to be the first Negro singer engaged by the Metropolitan, Miss Anderson?"

"One is speechless with happiness."

"Why do you usually use the word 'one' or 'we' instead

134

of 'I,' Miss Anderson?" another newspaper reporter asked her.

"Because the longer one lives," said Marian, "the surer one is that the 'I' in it is very small. There is nothing one has done alone. The composers, the people who make the pianos, the accompanist, the Lord who gives us the breath, make possible anything one does."

Pencils flew over notebooks. More questions. "Do you expect difficulty with the role?" "Are your colleagues pleasant to work with?" "Are you planning—"

"No—yes—"

"Enough!" Mr. Graf waved reporters away. "This is a rehearsal!" he said, enunciating each word clearly. "Not a press conference."

Marian bent over her caldron and stirred vigorously. Once again the music started, and her magnificent voice filled the empty cavern of the Opera House.

"Clutch your fist," called Mr. Graf. "Good. Now open it. Fine."

"After photographers had left," said *The New York Times*, "it was just another rehearsal at the Met. Although Marian Anderson had nothing to say on the subject, one knew it was exactly the way she would have wanted it."

Acting in opera stirred up memories of acting in a Camp Fire show as a little girl and then as a high school girl, attending plays presented by a troupe of fine Negro actors, . . . and when she got older, acting out whole operatic scenes with Boghetti. She enjoyed the excitement of working in opera, the stimulation of rehearsing with other great voices, and the "family feeling" and interchange of ideas.

"At the Met," she said, "I had to stretch my hours to crowd in more activity, and somehow it caused the blood to race through me with new meaning. I felt incredibly alive, able to do extra tasks for the first time in my life. I even got my letters answered!"

January 7, 1955, was opening night. The Metropolitan Opera House was ablaze with lights. Everyone, from the most beautifully gowned women in the Diamond Horseshoe to the last standee in the gallery under the gold ceiling, felt the electric excitement in the air. All openings are exciting. This one was special.

In the center box with Sol Hurok sat Mrs. Anna Anderson, Marian's mother; sisters, Ethel and Alyce; and husband, Orpheus Fisher. Throughout the audience were other Negroes, many of whom had never been to an opera before.

Houselights dimmed. The conductor appeared, made his way through the orchestra pit, mounted his stand. A hush . . . a rap of the baton . . . a moment of silence . . . the overture. When the famous golden curtains rose on the second scene, Marian was onstage, dressed in rags and a wild black wig, stirring her smoking caldron of "magic brew." There was a burst of applause, followed by a standing ovation. The conductor stopped the orchestra to allow the demonstration to end naturally. When all was quiet, Marian sang her opening aria.

"At first," said Critic Olin Downes, "she wavered a little, no doubt under the special tensions of the occasion . . . but before the air was finished, she demonstrated the same musicianship and instinct for dramatic communication she had long demonstrated on concert stage. And the climax of the scene when Ulrica prophesizes that Riccardo will die *'d'un amica'*—by the hand of a friend—was sung with such meaning that she stamped herself forever in the memory of all who listened."

When it was over, outburst followed outburst, curtain call followed curtain call. "No solo bows" was the new policy at the Met, but the audience insisted. "Anderson! Anderson! Anderson!" they called, and her fellow singers nudged her onstage for a moment alone.

Later she received newspaper people, friends, and family in her dressing room. And when the last flashbulb had popped, the last reporter been answered, the last flower put in a vase, Marian's mother stood on tiptoe, kissed her daughter, and said simply, "We thank the Lord."

136

In January, 1955, at the Metropolitan Opera House, Miss Anderson takes a curtain call following a thrilling opening-night performance.

Since Marian's debut, many other Negro artists have appeared with the Metropolitan Opera—Robert McFerrin, Gloria Davy, Mattiwilda Dobbs (a Marian Anderson scholarship winner), Martina Arroyo, George Shirley, and Leontyne Price. On the floor of the Grand Tier stands a bronze bust of Marian Anderson.

Marian sang Ulrica with the Metropolitan at the Philadelphia Academy of Music too. In a way the opening in her hometown was an even bigger thrill. "Marian Anderson came home in glory," said *The Philadelphia Inquirer*. Seated in the audience sharing that glory were some of the same people who had dropped pennies in the collection box for "The Fund for Marian's Future."

"When one was a little girl here in Philadelphia, one dreamed of singing with the Met at the Academy," she said at the Mayor's reception in her honor. "Tonight, the dream came true."

"Will you sing another role at the Met?" someone asked.

"First, one must learn this role better," was the reply. The Met had asked her to sing the role next season, and she would.

"Do you plan to continue your operatic career indefinitely?"

No, came the reply and as for switching from concert stage to opera, it was far too late for that.

When her first Metropolitan season ended, she was back on the concert stage again, this time on a spring tour with the Israel Philharmonic. Opera had stimulated her to a pitch of excitement. The pioneer country of Israel did not let her down. She had tea with the President and Prime Minister; attended a traditional Passover Seder like those her Jewish grandfather used to tell her about; made pilgrimages to holy places mentioned in her beloved spirituals; sang in a huge outdoor amphitheater in a kibbutz, or communal settlement. "Syria was so close to that kibbutz," she said, "the Arabs were notified of the concert ahead of time, lest the commotion make them think something more ominous was afoot!"

In Tel Aviv, she spoke to many young Israeli musicians and

was so impressed with their ideas that she established a scholarship for promising young Israeli singers.[4] From Tel Aviv she left for the city of Haifa. Halfway there, she turned in dismay to the director of the Israel Philharmonic and the other musicians in the car.

"Gentlemen," she said, "my dress for tonight's concert is in Tel Aviv." She had left it hanging on the closet door in her hotel room, planning to carry it on her lap to avoid pressing it in Haifa.

"The gentlemen of the Israel Philharmonic behaved as if dresses left behind were routine," she said later. Luckily, it was a short distance between the two cities, and the dress was delivered by messenger in plenty of time.

After Israel she was off to Morocco, Tunisia, and Spain with a stopover in Paris to appear again with the Israel Philharmonic. Mr. Hurok happened to be in Paris at the time, and he and Marian dined at his favorite restaurant.

"Anyone who knows him," Marian said, "knows that he is a marvelous host, and has a gourmet's knowledge of the best eating places in most parts of the world."

It was twenty years since their first meeting in Paris, and they had a fine time reminiscing about their "artistic partnership."

"I am sure," Marian said, "there have not been many relationships of this sort as amicable and gratifying." Perhaps how they handled contracts shows best the faith they had in each other. At first, they had both signed long, detailed contracts. After a while, when a new one arrived at Marian's home, she would put it aside, meaning to read and sign it "later." Somehow, she always forgot. "I wouldn't recommend this practice for every singer," she said, her eyes twinkling, "but that has been *our* way."

Since the first night they had met, Marian felt that Mr.

---

[4] Prizes were awarded to: Aharon Cohen, bass; Shmaya Ashkenazi, lyric tenor; Shulamith Shapiro, coloratura soprano; and Malka Ofrat, dramatic soprano.

Hurok had handled her career with utmost consideration and taste. "There was dignity in all things," she said, "in the publicity, and in the auspices he approved for appearances. Never did he accept an offer simply for a quick fee. He was more concerned whether or not a concert was right for me. And best of all, he took a deep personal interest in my career. Mr. Hurok is not just a manager, of course, but a courageous impresario, who takes chances whenever he believes in an artist."

After Paris, Marian returned home to a summer of rest on the farm with King. The following season there were appearances with the Met again, a spring tour of Latin America, and a return engagement to sing at Lewisohn Stadium in New York. Over thirty years had passed since her first appearance there as winner of the Stadium Contest. The voice still glows, said Taubman in *The New York Times,* and the audience would not go home.

There is much to enjoy on the farm in Connecticut.

15

FOR years people on every continent had admired Marian, not only for her art, but for her faith, courage, and the dignity with which she had met indignities. In fall, 1957, her country called on her. In Asia, new underdeveloped countries had been blanketed with troupes of entertainers. Our State Department, eager to send our best, sent Marian Anderson. Her instructions were brief: "You are not a propagandist. Just be yourself."

So Marian and her accompanist started a journey covering twelve countries and thirty-five thousand miles, from the thirty-eighth parallel to the equator. The Columbia Broadcasting System sent along a team of television technicians to photograph the historic tour for the folks at home.

Arriving at the Korean front by helicopter, Marian sang in a huge amphitheater deep in the Korean hills for an audience that included soldiers from Turkey, Greece, Britain, Thailand, France, and Korea, as well as GI's. Her flirtatious wink at the end of "Home Sweet Home" proved the magazine *Musical America* right, when they called hers "the best wink in the business."

In Seoul, capital of the Korean Republic, Marian was given an honorary degree from Ewha Women's University. "You are one of the great artists," said Helen Kim, the university's president. "You are respected as a leader among women. Your success against great odds has encouraged others in their struggle for justice and human rights. You stand as an example of Christian service to mankind."

Marian acknowledged the degree in the way she knew best. She sang: "He's Got the Whole World in His Hands."

Next stop was Saigon, in Vietnam, where a group of school children met her plane, singing Rodgers and Hammerstein's "Getting to Know You," in their newly learned English. On Sunday morning, she prayed with the Vietnamese people in a little village church; then, accompanied by an organ hundreds of years old, she sang "Let My People Go."

Miss Anderson sings at the Ewha Women's University, Seoul, South Korea, where she received an honorary doctorate of music.

From Saigon she continued on to Bangkok, capital of
Thailand, where the King had risen from his throne to greet
a foreign dignitary only a few times in his life. He stood up
for Marian Anderson. In Thailand, she visited schools, told the
children about Abraham Lincoln's Emancipation Proclama-
tion, and sang the spirituals of her people.

She visited Singapore; Taipei, Formosa; and Hong Kong,
where eight thousand people heard her in a single concert.
She journeyed next to Burma. Here Prime Minister U Nu
was among her backstage admirers. "Miss Anderson," he said,
"your performance tonight was a rare combination of good
voice, good technique, and good dramatic acting. The beauty
and charm of your mind are fully expressed in your dazzling
eyes and childlike lips."

Then came Ceylon, and the brand-new nation, Federation
of Malaya, or Malaysia, a melting pot of Chinese, Indians,
Malayans, and Eurasians. On the day their flag was first raised
in the United Nations, Marian sang at a boys' school in Kuala
Lumpur, the capital. "There is no doubt in my mind," she

*In Burma, congratulations came from Premier U Nu
and his wife.*

said to the boys, "that some of you who sit here today have the destiny of this new country in your hands. It is so very important," she said, "that you not let little things like hate and fear destroy you, restrict you from being the kind of big person you could be."

Boys with skins ranging from blond to bronze listened to her sing Rodgers and Hammerstein's "You've Got to Be Taught to Hate." They laughed with her, sang with her, applauded, and begged for more. And that evening, for the first time, the new Malayan anthem was sung by a foreign artist—Marian Anderson. "A mark of deep respect for our newborn nation," said the Kuala Lumpur newspaper.

On they went to Pakistan, and Bombay, India, where she sang with the Bombay City Orchestra, the only symphony between Tokyo and Tel Aviv. In July, four months before

A tour to Bombay, India, included a performance with the Bombay City Orchestra.

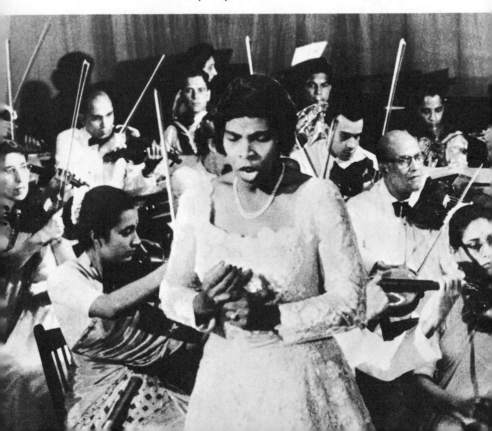

leaving home, she had received word that a newly formed Western symphony in Bombay would like to accompany her, if she could send them one of her scores to practice. She was delighted, and several pounds of Western music went eastward by mail. The conductor of the orchestra was a lawyer from Goa. The string section was composed of clerks, civil servants, housewives, teachers, doctors; the percussionist was an able-bodied seaman complete with turban and long, black beard; and Indian sailors and policemen made up the woodwind section.

From Bombay they proceeded to New Delhi. On the day of her concert, correspondent A. M. Rosenthal wrote to *The New York Times:* "The big thing to do in New Delhi today was to find someone with enough pull to get you into the Marian Anderson concert. . . . Just about the time members of the American Women's Club got the posters distributed, it was time to paste 'Full House' stickers on them. . . . Juggling the twelve hundred tickets was a major exercise in diplomacy."

Prime Minister Nehru was among the lucky ones to get into the hall.

Before returning home, Marian Anderson was the first foreigner ever invited to speak in old Delhi at the memorial to India's saint, Mahatma Gandhi, who during his lifetime had sent many inspiring messages to the Negroes of America.

Everywhere Marian went, there were interviews, photographs, questions. Questions about everything from baseball to the atom bomb to the Lincoln Memorial Concert. She was never too tired or rushed to answer slowly, calmly, with dignity. Back home Negro children were being stoned when they tried to enter white schools in Little Rock, Arkansas, and newspapers throughout the world carried the shameful story.

"Would you like to sing for the segregationist Governor Faubus?" she was asked by a journalist in Burma.

"If it could help at all," she answered, "if Governor Faubus would be in the frame of mind to accept it for what it is, from what he could get from it, I would be very delighted to do it."

As a Negro, she was vitally concerned with what was going on at Little Rock. As an American, she was embarrassed for her country.

"Our Fair Lady," the Indian press called her. "A brilliant singer and a great woman," said the *Manila Record*. "Our secret weapon," said General Alfred M. Gruenther, who had been concerned with the effect of Soviet propaganda on new nations. "We need more Marian Andersons."

At home her countrymen saw the tour on television on Edward Murrow's *See It Now*. "Probably the most widely applauded show in TV history," said *Newsweek*. It drew unanimous raves from critics, won acclaim in editorial pages from coast to coast, including the Deep South. "Miss Anderson has done this country a great service," said the *Atlanta Constitution*. And the *Daily News* in Greensboro, North Carolina: "Marian Anderson in Asia was worth more than two hundred sputniks in space."

Marian impressed the peoples of Asia, and the peoples of Asia impressed Marian. "I had not been taught enough about them," she said. "Cities were dots on maps . . . and sort of impersonal. Then one went there, saw the buildings, and the seething mobs of people, sang to them, talked to people as intelligent as one finds anywhere. There are great areas of the world where people need to meet Americans of equal intelligence, with common interests. Then many misconceptions will be cleared away."

The State Department was so pleased with the job she had done that they distributed prints of the *See It Now* telecast to U.S. Information Service posts in seventy-nine countries. It was shown in native movie houses, schools, clubs, churches, and mobile units in tropical jungles and deserts throughout the entire world!

President Eisenhower realized that the peoples of Asia didn't admire Marian for her voice alone. Like everyone else, they admired her understanding, her ability to communicate with people, her sincere desire to understand the other per-

146

Miss Anderson was appointed by President Eisenhower to serve as United States Delegate to the United Nations.

son's point of view. And so, in July, 1958, he appointed her a member of the United States Delegation to the United Nations.

"There is something special about it . . . ," said *The New York Times*. "The choice may be construed as a recognition of her own unique worth. We like to think, however, that it is rather a way in which the United States does honor to the world organization."

Marian postponed concerts scheduled for fall, when the UN was in session. At 9 A.M. on September 18, she entered her UN office for the first time. "I like it here," she said.

She was assigned to the Trusteeship Committee, a special group concerned with the well-being of peoples under UN trusteeship. It became her responsibility to study the situation in Togoland and the Cameroons, newly liberated countries on the west coast of Africa, and to present her findings to the committee.

147

"Marian Anderson was a most effective member of the U.S. Delegation," said Henry Cabot Lodge, Chief Delegate. "She handled all topics assigned her with great skill, and, on the personal plane, was extremely well liked and respected by all."

No doubt part of that respect stemmed from the fact that Marian was courageous enough to speak her mind, even when her opinions differed with the rest of her delegation's. Later, she said, "I understand better, I think, than others serving with me, a great many things that motivated the hopes and pleas and demands of the little nations, particularly those whose people are dark-skinned. How much my people could contribute to our Government's understanding of those other nations! But, at the same time, my Government is learning more about my people, because it's concerned now with the world. So this is good, good for my country and my people."

Said fellow delegate Senator Mike Mansfield of Montana: "Marian Anderson worked diligently, unceasingly; she made her views known. Her contribution to the success which the UN achieved at that assembly were many. She was a fine colleague; she attended to all her duties; she did her homework well. She was articulate and represented our country with honor and distinction."

Irving Salomon, another fellow delegate, added that if character, charm, and personality make noble women, Marian Anderson would certainly be listed high. He continued that, with the possible exception of Eleanor Roosevelt, he knew of no other woman who has earned the respect, esteem, and affection of so many people.

Author Vincent Sheean was eager to see Marian in her new role. "One day I lunched with her in the delegates' dining room at the UN," he said. "Marian was absolutely imperial in her grace, her kindness, her attentive and humble grandeur. . . . At one point during lunch a very handsome young man, who must have been an Arab, darted across the room and took Marian's right hand. . . . She turned without a tremor and lifted her hand for the young man to kiss. He did not say a word. He darted away. Marian returned to her coffee. 'Who is that?' I asked. 'I do not know,' she said.

"There have been a considerable number of times," said Mr. Sheean, "when my mind has been forced to consider Marian Anderson not only as a contralto and musician, not only as an artist and patriot, not only as a supreme example of what we are on earth to prove (the American dream), but also as something which has nothing to do with the United States or the American dream. It is the reality . . . of the soul. Marian is a sort of proof of the immortality of the soul. . . . The only human being of whom she really reminds me is no king, queen, pope, or president . . . she reminds me of Mahatma Gandhi."

CHAPTER

16

THE thirteenth session of the UN over, Marian resumed her concert career, and in January, 1959, she was elected to the American Academy of Arts and Sciences, founded during the American Revolution "to advance the interest, honor, dignity, and happiness of a free, independent, and virtuous people," as the founders of the Academy expressed it. She was in good company. The Academy's membership, limited to those of highest achievement, included inventor Alexander Graham Bell; poet Henry Wadsworth Longfellow; astronomer Maria Mitchell; explorer Vilhjalmur Stefansson; and Marian's old friend, Roland Hayes.

On January 21, 1961, came another never-to-be-forgotten day in a life filled with memorable days. Marian, singing "The Star-spangled Banner," opened the inauguration ceremonies of President John F. Kennedy. Televiewers throughout the world saw her rise from her seat beside Robert Frost, move to the platform, lift her voice in song, and afterward congratulate our new President. The following November she met President Kennedy again—twice in the same month. On November 22, he and West German Chancellor Adenauer greeted her as one of the founders of the Freedom from Hunger Foundation, an organization working with the UN to help feed underprivileged people everywhere. And on November 29, she sang a gala program to raise funds for the National Cultural Center, in Washington, D.C., and the President and

150

Mrs. John Fitzgerald Kennedy were on the same platform.

Before she left for her first tour of Australia, another invitation came from the White House—to visit with President Kennedy, lunch with wives of Cabinet members, and attend a concert at the State Department Auditorium. Mrs. Robert Kennedy, who drove Marian to the White House that day, sang to the singer all the way down Pennsylvania Avenue!

The year 1963 was an active one in the cause of civil rights. Some Negroes felt that Marian, as a prominent member of their race, should join in demonstrations, speak out against discrimination. But although Marian believed peaceful demonstration necessary to advance the cause, she felt the best way for her to fight was by singing.

In November, 1963, she represented all descendants of slavery at the rededication of the National Cemetery at Get-

President Kennedy greets Marian Anderson and Franz Rupp before a concert at the State Department Auditorium, Washington, D.C.

151

tysburg, where Lincoln first gave his Gettysburg Address. She often participated in civil rights benefits, and in July, 1963, she gave a benefit lawn party on the grounds of her Connecticut farm. Said the Danbury, Connecticut, *News-Times:*

Despite 90-degree temperatures, guests gathered beneath a green and white striped canopy to sample canapes and punch, to chat, and to contribute. Among notables attending were actor Frederick March and his wife, Florence Eldredge, . . . photographer Edward Steichen, mystery authors Rex Stout and Manfred Lee, playwright Joseph Hayes, and State Treasurer Gerald Lamb, the first Negro to be elected to high office in Connecticut.

That afternoon, three thousand dollars was raised for the NAACP Emergency Freedom Fund.

"We need protest, and we have to have it," said Rev. J. H. Jackson, president of the National Baptist Convention of America, "but a Marian Anderson, a Roland Hayes, a Negro who has accomplished some creative excellence, can achieve more than a thousand sit-ins."

After President Kennedy's assassination, Marian was asked to sing at a special memorial, held at the New York City Hall Plaza. Said *The New York Times:*

It was a blend of eloquence . . . prayer . . . music sung by Marian Anderson . . . in a spot where nearly one hundred years ago, the body of Lincoln lay in state. "What President Kennedy did in the Civil Rights field," said Roy Wilkins, Executive Secretary, NAACP, "he did for people, for the colored victims and the white victimizers." . . . Then Marian Anderson, her eyes closed, her voice echoing through the plaza and reechoing beyond the skyscrapers, sang three Negro spirituals, "Let Us Break Bread Together," "Hear De Lam's a-Crying," and "Ride On, King Jesus." There was none of the spirit she demonstrated when she sang at President Kennedy's inauguration.

The crowd, obeying the wishes of Robert W. Dowling, cultural executive of the city, . . . did not applaud—but it was not easy.

152

Three days after the memorial on December 6, 1963, Marian again visited the White House. In the State Dining Room before members of the Supreme Court, the Cabinet, and Congress, President Johnson bestowed on her the highest civilian honor the President can give in peacetime—the Presidential Medal of Freedom.

Other winners of the medal included Negro statesman Dr. Ralphe Bunche; educator James Conant; Supreme Court Justice Felix Frankfurter; and cellist Pablo Casals. President Kennedy had chosen the award winners himself—all but one. He was awarded the medal posthumously.

"This is a moment of great pride," said President Johnson, "following moments of utmost sorrow, anguish, and shame. In Mr. Kennedy's assassination, we encountered in its full horror, man's capacity for hate and destruction. It is time to turn once more to pursuits of honor . . . excellence . . . and achievement that have always marked the true direction of the American people." He read the first citation: "Marian Anderson, artist and citizen . . . she has ennobled her race and her country, while her voice has enthralled the world."

On December 6, 1963, President Johnson congratulated Miss Anderson following the presentation of the Presidential Medal of Freedom.

17

S OMEONE once asked Marian what she considered the greatest moment in her life. Was it when Toscanini took her hand and said she had the greatest voice of the century? The first time she sang at the White House? The moment she was presented with the Spingarn Medal? The Bok Award? The Presidential Medal of Freedom? When she learned Sibelius had dedicated his song "Solitude" to her? The Lincoln Memorial Concert? Singing at the Metropolitan Opera? Her appointment to the UN?

Without hesitation, Marian replied: "The happiest day in my life was when I told my mother she didn't need to work anymore."

"It is the pleasantest thing in the world to go into that home and feel its happiness," said Marian. "They are all comfortable, and they cherish and protect one another. When I phone from out of town late at night and speak to my sister, I ask whether Mama has gone to bed, and I am told, 'She is right here,' I remind Mama that she should be getting to bed early and I can hear her laughing softly as she says, 'Right away, right away.' "

"My little girl," Marian called her mother, and for almost forty years, Anna Delilah Anderson was a familiar figure in the musical world, sitting quietly in concert halls, enjoying what must be the supreme pride of motherhood. On January 10, 1964, at the age of eighty-nine, she died in South Philadelphia in the same house she and her daughter had bought almost half a century before. Mrs. Anderson, Alyce, and Ethel might have moved away from that modest house long ago. The neighborhood had become run-down; the location was far from desirable in terms of real estate. To them, it was home.

When Ethel married, she and her husband bought the adjoining house, so Mrs. Anderson had the joy of watching her only grandchild grow to manhood. "Perhaps," Marian said, "she felt familiar sensations as she watched Jim, the high school boy, go off on trips with his jazz band, and earn money on his own."

Marian accepted her mother's death with the same faith Mama herself had instilled in her. "I am only glad she lived long enough to realize her three girls appreciated the sacrifices she'd made for them," she said, "and that I could do a little for her in return."

"What is it like to be a Negro in a white world?" Marian's friend, author Emily Kimbrough asked her, when they'd been friends for twenty-five years. And their long talk inspired Miss Kimbrough to write an article about it for *Ladies' Home Journal*.

"Sometimes," said Marian, "it's like having a hair across your cheek. You can't find it with your hand, but you keep brushing at it because the feel of it is irritating."

"When did you first become aware of it?" asked Emily.

Marian told her about the day at the music school, and the receptionist who'd said, "We don't take colored," slamming the window in her face.

"Well," said Emily, "at least, now, you're recognized wherever you go, so you're not subjected to that 'hair across your cheek.'"

Marian smiled. "Remember yesterday," she said, "it was five when I left you, and I hailed a cab. The driver didn't pass me by, and was friendly and talkative. He hoped I'd done a good day's work, he said, and that my 'boss lady' was satisfied.

155

You see, he assumed that any Negro going uptown at that time of day was a maid, treating herself to a cab to ease her tired feet."

Marian told Emily about an incident that had happened the year before at a California hotel, where she had stayed many times.

"We're delighted to have you back," the desk clerk had said when she arrived. "I'm coming to your concert tonight."

"Thank you," said Marian. "I hope you enjoy it." After signing the register, she crossed the lobby to the elevator.

"The service elevator for you," said the elevator operator, as he placed his arm across the doorway.

"So you see, being Marian Anderson doesn't always make such a difference," Marian said. "White people who don't know individuals lump Negroes under a general category: domestic, train porter, whatever."

At one point in their conversation, Emily burst out angrily: "It's a wonder to me," she said, "that every Negro in our society isn't neurotic. If I had to put up my arm, so to speak, to ward off some discrimination that happened every day— being passed by a bus driver, or waited on last in a department store, or ignored altogether—I think I'd either stay indoors, or go, not with my arm up, but with my *fists* up!"

Marian smiled at her friend's outburst. "I can't speak for how other Negroes feel," she said. "I expect there are plenty of neurotics. But then there are others so busy working for the betterment of our people that they have no time to be turned aside by small annoyances. And I suppose others are just plain discouraged; and some are so indifferent they sit back and let others cut a path for them. But when those working for the Negro's betterment look back, they can't help seeing that the path has come a long way from where it started. It's wider and clearer; so it's worthwhile for them to keep pushing ahead and cutting down obstacles."

"Where do you belong, Marian?" asked Emily.

"I'm a believer," said Marian, "in God and the ultimate

goodness of man. I believe that one day it's going to come over a lot of people who are shouting against equality for the Negro, that association with him is just as easy as believing is for me. You see, I care so much about my country. I've sung almost all over the world, and I've loved the opportunity. But east, west, home is best. Only I worry about it—once a man visiting my class at school said, 'You can't hold something down without bending over, or in some way lowering yourself. You have to get down to that same level.' I'm so proud of my country, I hate to think of it stooping or bending to hold down some of its people."

"Do you think equality will be accomplished by the laws of school integration, housing, employment, and so on?" asked Emily.

Marian shook her head. "Not by those laws alone, as wonderful as they are. They've certainly widened the path, and carried it way ahead. But you have to accomplish the little things too. Wipe away once and for all that hair across the Negro's cheek. It's as important as all the laws. You can't build a chimney from the top!"

"Marian Anderson has never asked for indiscriminate love for the minority races," said Harold Schonberg in an article in *The New York Times Magazine*. "She wants understanding."

"Understanding," Marian said, "does not mean you have to embrace the Negro or white person. The Negro or the white person must be judged as an individual, with all his goodness or badness, and the color of his skin makes no difference. He who made us all did not make any mistake when he made us of a different color."

THREE o'clock, Easter Sunday afternoon, April 19, 1965 . . . Marian Anderson's Farewell Concert at Carnegie Hall. . . .

"She stepped across the stage," wrote Bernard Weinraub, in *The New York Times,* and the applause rose from the audience in a sweeping, throbbing wave.

"Her eyes glistening, her lips in a tight smile, she whispered, 'Thank you, thank you.' . . . Suddenly, dramatically, the entire audience—2,900 persons—stood, clapping, cheering, and acclaiming the woman onstage—Marian Anderson."

The concert over, Marian Anderson in a fur-trimmed scarlet gown stood backstage, hands clasped before her, head cocked, listening to the ovation ringing through the hall.

"One more encore," said Sol Hurok, tapping his cane against a fire extinguisher. "One more."

She had already sung four. "No," she said, "it's finished."

"Then," wrote Jimmy Breslin, in the *New York Herald Tribune,* "Marian Anderson turned her back on the stage . . . and, her arms filled with roses, climbed the stairs and talked about what it is like to finish a career that began forty years ago in Philadelphia, and reached out to the world.

" 'Now,' she said, 'I'm going to be a homemaker.' "

"They're still clapping, Miss Anderson," one of Hurok's staff called.

She didn't move.

"Don't hold her back," Sol Hurok requested of reporters on the steps. "The public are not leaving."

"Oh," said Marian Anderson, "then I had better go down again."

And once more, Marian Anderson moved onto the stage at Carnegie Hall. The lights went up. People shouted over clapping hands. Photographers leaned onstage and snapped her picture.

But although her recital career was officially over, plans were already afoot for her to appear on "extraordinary occasions."

"She cannot retire. The world will not allow it," said Sol Hurok when the ovation finally subsided, and Miss Anderson received reporters, friends, and well-wishers in her dressing room.

Marian Anderson smiled. "I'm going to be a homemaker," she repeated, glancing at her husband. "And I hope to do something for children—perhaps help provide them with foster homes. I want to roll up my sleeves. I want to do something with my hands, and my heart, and my soul."

Enthusiastic audiences respond to the gracious artist.

ACKNOWLEDGMENTS

The author wishes to thank the following for their assistance in gathering material for this book:

Henry Lee Moon, National Association for the Advancement of Colored People

Anne Gordon, Metropolitan Opera Association

May M. Dowell and Joseph Levine, Columbia Broadcasting System

Madeline G. Mitchell and Alice V. Smith, United Nations Visitors' Service

Marjorie Reitz, U.S. Mission to the United Nations

Henry Cabot Lodge, former Head, U.S. Delegation to the UN, and Ambassador to Saigon

Senator Mike J. Mansfield, U.S. Senate, former Delegate to the UN

Herman Phlegger, former Delegate to the UN

Mrs. Oswald B. Lord, former Delegate to the UN

Irving Salomon, former Delegate to the UN

Jessie Janjigian, World Peace Foundation, Boston

Mrs. Nora Sanborn, American Institute of Public Opinion (Gallup Poll)

161

Samuel Jochanan, American-Israel Cultural Foundation

Stephen Collins, Editor, Danbury *News-Times*

Jerry Miller and Herbert Helman, Radio Corporation of America

Michael Sweeley, Hurok Attractions, Inc.

Alexandra Oleson, American Academy of Arts and Sciences

Samuel Malkin, Principal, William Penn High School, Philadelphia

Special thanks to Roland Hayes and Mrs. Hayes for their gracious hospitality and remembrances; Orpheus Fisher, Mrs. Mary Dolan, Miss Anderson's secretary; and, of course, to Miss Anderson herself. Thanks, too, to the Free Library of Philadelphia, the Boston Public Library, and the Free Library of Newton, Massachusetts, and all librarians therein, who are forever helping me track down elusive material. Extra special thanks to my family, for their patience.

SELECTED BIBLIOGRAPHY

BOOKS

Adams, Russell L., *Great Negroes, Past and Present*. Afro-American Publishing Company, Inc., 1964.

Anderson, Marian, *My Lord, What a Morning* (autobiography). The Viking Press, Inc., 1956.

Anderson, Marian, "My Mother's Gift—Grace Before Greatness," in *Faith Made Them Champions*, ed. by Norman Vincent Peale. Prentice-Hall, Inc., 1955.

Bakeless, Katherine, *In the Big Time*. J. B. Lippincott Company, 1953.

Bontemps, Arna, *Story of the Negro*. Alfred A. Knopf, Inc., 1958.

Clapper, Olive Ewing, *Washington Tapestry*. McGraw-Hill Book Company, Whittlesey House, 1946.

Downes, Irene, ed., *Olin Downes on Music*. Simon and Schuster, Inc., 1957.

Embree, Edwin R., *Thirteen Against the Odds*. The Viking Press, Inc., 1944.

Ewen, David, *Men and Women Who Made Music*. Merlin Press, Inc., 1949.

Helm, MacKinley, *Angel Mo' and Her Son, Roland Hayes*. Little Brown and Company, 1942.

Hughes, Langston, *Famous American Negroes*. Dodd, Mead & Company, Inc., 1954.

Hurok, Sol (and Ruth Goode), *Impresario, A Memoir*. Random House, Inc., 1946.

Johnson, James W., *Book of American Negro Spirituals*. The

Viking Press, Inc., 1925.

Karsh, Yousuf, *Portraits of Greatness*. Thomas Nelson & Sons, 1959.

Matz, Mary Jane, *Opera Stars in the Sun*. Farrar, Straus & Cudahy, Inc., 1955.

Metropolitan Opera Guild, Incorporated, *Opera Cavalcade*, 1938.

Peltz, Mary Ellis, *The Magic of the Opera*. Frederick A. Praeger, Inc., 1960.

Richardson, Ben, *Great American Negroes*. The Thomas Y. Crowell Co., 1956.

Rothery, Agnes, *New York Today*. Prentice-Hall, Inc., 1951.

Sheean, Vincent, *Between the Thunder and the Sun*. Random House, Inc., 1943.

Sheean, Vincent, *First and Last Love*. Random House, Inc., 1956.

Stevenson, J., *Singing to the World*. Encyclopaedia Britannica, Inc., 1963.

Taubman, Howard, *Music on My Beat*. Simon and Schuster, Inc., 1943.

Thomas, H. and D., *Fifty Great Modern Lives*. Hanover House, 1936.

Thurman, Howard, *Deep River*. Harper & Row, Publishers, Inc., 1955.

Vehanen, K., *Marian Anderson*. McGraw-Hill Book Company, Whittlesey House, 1941.

MAGAZINES

Anderson, Marian, "My Life in a White World," as told to Emily Kimbrough, *Ladies' Home Journal*, September, 1960.

Anderson, Marian, "Some Reflections on Singing," as told to Rose Heylbut, *Etude*, October, 1939.

Bronson, Arthur, "Marian Anderson," *The American Mercury*, September, 1945.

Davenport, Marcia, "Music Will Out," *Collier's*, December 3, 1938.

Eyer, R., "Anderson Debut in Masked Ball Makes Met History," *Musical America*, January 15, 1955.

Hawkins, William, "Marian Anderson Says Farewell," *Musical America*, September, 1964.

Hemming, R., "Voice of the Century at the U.N.," *Senior Scholastic*, October 31, 1958.

Hughes, A., "Something Eternal," *Musical America*, February, 1959.

Kaladin, I., "Miss Anderson Makes History," *Saturday Review of Literature*, January 22, 1955.

Sargeant, W., "Anderson at the Met," *The New Yorker*, January 15, 1955.

Sedgwick, Ruth, "Over Jordan," *The Christian Century*, February 21, 1940 (also *Reader's Digest*, March, 1940).

Shayon, R., "The Lady from Philadelphia," *Saturday Review of Literature*, January 18, 1958.

Schonberg, Harold, "The Other Voice of Marian Anderson," *The New York Times Magazine*, August 10, 1958.

Taubman, H., "Voice of a Race," *The New York Times Magazine*, April 6, 1941.

Woolf, S. J., "Marian Anderson's Recipe for Success," *The New York Times Magazine*, December 30, 1942.

Zegri, A., "Song and Statesmanship," *Americas*, February, 1959.

My teen-aged daughter Paula, helping me type this manuscript, looked up from her typewriter recently and said: "Is this all true, Mother? Or did you fictionalize?"

It's all true, based on actual happenings. And fortunate, indeed, is the biographer who need not make up incidents to make exciting reading. Occasionally, toward the beginning of the book, I have switched the sequence of events a bit, but for the most part, I have simply reported what took place, using actual dialogue whenever possible, as remembered by Marian Anderson herself or someone who was there.

What is she really like—this woman who, in 1964, was voted one of the most admired women in the United States for the *sixth* time . . . this woman who has received honorary degrees from Smith, Howard University, Fordham, Mount Holyoke, and so many other colleges and universities it would take pages to list them. Kings have risen to greet her. Presidents have sought her out. Two high schools, a recreation center, a rose, and hundreds of children are named after her.

I had read reams about her. I knew not only the facts—the dates, the events—but I'd tracked down personal clues too, such as how she doesn't always tell her husband the price of a gown; how she phones him every night when she's away from home; how, when she can't get her hair done, she wears a wig onstage. I knew that one of her dogs had once bitten a passerby. I knew the date she had gotten her driver's license;

167

how she had cultivated a taste for epicurean food. I'd played her records thin—in short, except for practical purposes (like making supper for my family), I had been Marian Anderson for months. Now, I stood at the door of her apartment and rang the bell. The door opened almost at once. Standing before me, with a welcoming smile, was a pretty Negro woman with the largest, most expressive eyes imaginable. ("Perhaps it's just as well she closes them when singing," *Musical America* said, "because the audience might find it hard to concentrate on the music.") Her hair was combed in a wispy bang over her forehead, and in her mustard-yellow knit, she was a trim figure indeed.

For a moment, we looked at each other. I murmured something like "at last"—and we both laughed. Sensing my nervousness, perhaps, she took my hand, drew me inside, hung up my jacket, and led me to the sofa in front of a window overlooking Central Park. She was eager to help me however she could, she said. Tucking one leg under her, and looking amazingly girlish, she answered my questions slowly, thoughtfully, always ending with: "Is that what you need? Is that what you want?"

Her conversation is animated; her eyes quick to light with laughter. When she speaks of her mother—"her little girl," as she calls her, her eyes grow warm, soft. She calls her husband "her young man"; and when I mentioned her nephew, James, she glowed with pride and told me that the following week, he was conducting a concert for young people in New York.

Before the afternoon was over: "Tell me about yourself," she said. "Do you have children? What are they like?" And I told her how the day before, my son, Jeff, had told his friends *his* mother was interviewing Marian Anderson tomorrow! She laughed, relieved, I know, when I finally allowed the conversation to veer away from her. Although she is far too poised to show it outwardly, I have no doubt she finds it embarrassing to talk about herself—especially her honorary degrees.

168

(She's become Dr. Anderson more than thirty times, at this writing.) When you mention the degrees, she looks away a moment and says, "One doesn't know nearly enough—"

A month or so later, I went to Miss Anderson's Farewell Concert at Boston's Symphony Hall. As she walked onstage with her accompanist, she looked taller, somehow, than she did that day in her apartment. Her hairdo was higher— back-combed a bit on top, perhaps; in her apartment she had worn comfortable flats instead of heels—and, of course, her slim white, floor-length gown all contributed to the feeling of height. Her dignity, her stature, her confidence, her bearing, came from within. Standing in the curve of the piano before the golden pipes on the stage of Symphony Hall, she was in *her* world. She was as regal as the royalty for whom she has sung.

"But I thought she was dowdy," whispered a voice behind me. "She's stunning!"

"I thought she was older," whispered another. "How old *is* she, anyhow?"

Miss Anderson doesn't tell. And neither shall I. It really does not matter. She is ageless.

I had been early for the concert that Sunday afternoon, and I'd lingered in the lobby watching the audience assemble. Boston society arrived in chauffeur-driven limousines . . . political dignitaries alighted from cars with single-digit license plates. I recognized eminent musicians and spoke to Miss Anderson's old friend and inspiration, Roland Hayes, and his wife, whom I'd interviewed at their home in nearby Brookline. But perhaps the most stirring arrival of all was a frail young Negro woman who was lifted from her taxi into a wheelchair. She shivered, and as an usher wheeled her past, I heard him say, "Miss, it's so cold—you should be wearing a coat."

"Oh!" she said, her bright laughter echoing through the crowded lobby, "don't worry about *me*. This is the happiest day of my life. I'm going to hear Marian Anderson."

SHIRLEE P. NEWMAN was born in Boston, Massachusetts. Her family moved to California, when she was a teen-ager, and she attended Beverly Hills High School. Following graduation, she attended Sawyer's School of Business in West Los Angeles and later became an advertising copywriter for agencies in Los Angeles and San Francisco.

After moving to New York, she married Jackson J. Newman in 1946 and became a free-lance writer and photographer for trade publications. Mrs. Newman entered the field of juvenile writing when her children Paula and Jeff became old enough to enjoy having stories read to them.

At first she was a free-lance writer, selling stories and articles to *Child Life, Jack and Jill, Instructor, Grade Teacher, Scholastic Magazines, The American Girl,* and *Calling All Girls.* Later she became the Associate Editor of *Child Life.*

Mrs. Newman now spends her time in free-lance writing and is the author of nine juveniles, including MARIAN ANDERSON: LADY FROM PHILADELPHIA. Two of these juveniles were written in collaboration with Diane Sherman. Mrs. Newman feels that many of the original ideas for her articles and stories are inspired by her own children, their situations, interests, problems, as well as their school curricula.

174